Learning to Fly in Canada

Chris Hobbs

Detselig Enterprises Ltd.

Calgary, Alberta, Canada

Learning to Fly in Canada

© 2000 Chris Hobbs

Cataloguing in Publication Data

Hobbs, Chris, 1949-

Learning to fly in Canada

Includes index.

ISBN 1-55059-200-9

1. Airplanes - Piloting. 2. Private flying - Canada. 3. Airplanes - Piloting - Examinations, questions, etc. 4. Private flying - Canada - Examinations, questions, etc. I. Title.

TL713.C3H62 2000   629.132'5217'0971   C00-910173-X

Detselig Enterprises Ltd.

210-1220 Kensington Rd. N.W.

Calgary, AB T2N 3P5

Telephone: (403) 283-0900

Fax: (403) 283-6947

e-mail: temeron@telusplanet.net

www.temerondetselig.com

We acknowledge the financial support of the Government of Canada through the Book Industry Development Program (BPIDP) for our publishing activities.

ISBN: 1-55059-200-9

SAN: 115-0324

Printed in Canada

Cover design by Dean Macdonald & Alvin Choong

*This book is dedicated to
my primary flight instructors,
particularly Doc Saundby and John Bellocchi,
who taught me how to learn.*

Contents

Contents

Foreword

Earning a Private Pilot Licence could be your first step towards becoming a professional pilot or your only step to becoming a recreational one. While I hope that this book has something to offer both types of reader, it is written primarily for those who intend to fly for pleasure.

Books on learning to fly abound, but most assume that the reader has started flight training. They deal with the technical issues of getting an aircraft from A to B and landing successfully. This book is different, as it is for those considering starting training. Existing books also tend to be oriented towards flying in the USA or the UK and, while handling an aircraft doesn't differ from country to country, regulations and procedures do and continual reference to US regulations (FARs) can be both confusing and annoying. This book refers to few regulations, but those that it does mention are Canadian ones.

Learning to fly is hard work and it has its rewards and frustrations. I would like to think of you, after a lesson during which you have still failed to master a cross-wind landing or clean stall recovery, taking down this book and using it to rekindle your enthusiasm. I enjoy flying and hope that this pleasure comes through to you. In my primary training I came close to giving up a couple of times. I'm glad I didn't and hope that you don't.

I would like to thank my instructors, past and present, and the flying students, actual and prospective, who kindly read early drafts of this book and gave me their comments – in particular Elva Nilsen, Jannette Panel, Alison Hobbs (my navigator on many long flights), Mark Washer, Guy Duxbury, Steve Glasspool and Peter (Doc) Saundby. I would particularly like to thank Peter Ashwood-Smith, who contributed the section on aerobatics, and George McKenzie, who wrote about ultralights, both describing types of flying that I have not (yet) explored. The photographs in this book, unless otherwise noted, are the creation of David Mann, a very professional amateur photographer.

Chris Hobbs
Rockcliffe Flying Club
Rockcliffe Airport (CYRO)
Ottawa

Introduction

I have just returned from a short flight around Ottawa. There was no reason for flying today; visibility is poor, there is scratchy cloud at 2800 feet, preventing me from climbing to any great height, the air is bumpy, making the ride uncomfortable, and a strong gusty wind is blowing from the south, making landing on Rockcliffe's east/west runway a challenge. I flew for an hour or so, which cost me about $50. So why did I go? Even more puzzling, why did my wife accompany me? I didn't really need the practice and, with Ottawa and the rivers in view throughout our lazy circle, I didn't learn much about navigation.

We flew today because we knew that Gatineau Park, over which we've circled hundreds of times, would look different again. We went because of the freedom flying offers. Next week, weather permitting, we'll go further, over new country, but even a short sight-seeing trip almost within sight of home had newness to it. Pilots find excuses to fly: they'll fly for an hour "to warm up the oil before changing it." Last weekend a friend took his aircraft up for an hour or so "to dry it after it had been washed."

Flying and learning to fly are exciting and rewarding activities. Flying in Canada is a delight as clubs are numerous, airspace is largely open, it is comparatively cheap and the landscape is a seasonal wonder to look down upon.

This book is not intended to teach you how to control the aircraft: that you will learn from your Flight Instructor. Nor is it a book to cram you through the written examinations; there are several of those. Instead it is designed to be read in bed as you decide whether to start flight training and, if you've started and had a bad day, whether to continue. It explains some of the jargon and tries to dispel the myth that flying is difficult. Pilots like to think so, but frankly, they're wrong.

The rest of this chapter gives short answers to some of the questions I would like to have had answered at the beginning of my training. Some of these questions seem odd to experienced pilots. To them, flying into an unfamiliar airport, tying their aircraft down and driving away is second nature. To someone starting their training, even this simple activity raises lots of questions.

Like any hobby, flying has its own vocabulary. A glossary of much of this is included at the back of this book.

Will I be able to learn to fly?

It is commonly said that if you are physically fit and can drive a car, then you can learn to fly.

Does it matter that I have in-grown toe-nails, tennis elbow and bubonic plague?

The short answer is that I don't know. Before you are allowed to fly solo, you will have to be examined by an aviation medical examiner. He or she will advise you on the wisdom of flying with those toe-nails.

I suffer from motion-sickness; will I feel sick in the air?

Almost everyone who suffers from this acclimatizes successfully. Funnily enough, very few people feel sick when they're actually controlling the aircraft. I had a passenger turn green on me once and I asked him to steer the aircraft while I pretended to fumble for a map on the back seat and his normal color returned within a few minutes. There does, however, seem to be a strong correlation between people drinking soda pop immediately before flying and feeling queasy in the air. Flying on an empty stomach should also be avoided.

Does it matter that I'm color-blind?

Yes and no. I suffer from this condition and know that it will not stop you from getting a pilot's licence. It will, however, prevent you from flying at night. There is pressure on the authorities to relax this restriction, since it dates from the days when control towers routinely shone colored lights to indicate to pilots whether they could land or not. Most aircraft these days have radios and the colored lights are relegated to a cupboard. For the time being, however, you must resign yourself to flying only during daylight.

Will I fly on my own before I get my licence?

Certainly. This is an essential part of the flight training.

Will I have to talk on the radio?

Strictly speaking, if you choose your airports carefully, you can fly over most of Canada without having to use a radio at all. Some aircraft don't even have a radio.

However, it takes a lot of the fun and flexibility out of flying. If you don't use the radio, you won't be able to fly into, or even go close to, any medium or large airport. During your training, your instructor will insist on you using the radio and, once you start, any microphone fright will soon disappear. In fact, many low-time pilots become convinced that they are radio stars and use the microphone too much.

If you remember to engage your brain, and even rehearse what you are going to say, before pressing the Push-To-Talk switch, you should have no problems. If you invest in a hand-held radio, then you can sit at home and learn by listening to other pilots' radio techniques.

Aren't there a lot of difficult written examinations?

Just three and none is really difficult:

- 📖 a short examination, taken at your flying club, to demonstrate that you know how to use the radio;

- 📖 another short examination, again taken at your flying club, to demonstrate a basic understanding of air law;

- 📖 a longer examination, taken at a Transport Canada test site, to demonstrate that you are going to be a capable pilot.

These are all multiple-choice examinations and, if you are properly prepared, they are not difficult.

Isn't there a lot of mathematics to learn?

You are qualifying as a pilot, not as an aeronautical engineer. Arithmetic does enter into a few areas, in particular when finding the centre of gravity of a loaded aircraft, calculating runway distances and deciding in which direction to point the aircraft when flying in a wind. I have a degree in mathematics, so am probably not the best person to ask, but I've never known anyone unable to complete their licence because of their lack of mathematical aptitude.

Aren't there a lot of complex gauges and controls to understand?

The photograph on the next page shows the gauges and controls of a well-equipped small aircraft. At first glance there *are* a lot of gauges, but they break down into several groups: those associated with the aircraft's position (how high am I? how fast am I flying? in which direction am I flying?), those associated with the engine (how fast is it turning? how hot is the oil?) and those associated with the radios and navigation equipment. Your flight

Piper Cherokee GXBU's instruments.

instructor will probably start your training by getting you to ignore most of the instruments – you should, for example, be able to stay at a constant height without looking inside the aircraft. You will gradually be introduced to the more important gauges and you will probably teach yourself some of the navigation devices which don't form part of the Private Pilot test. The flight controls are even simpler – rudder pedals and a control column.

What will I be able to do when I get a licence?

There are two licences that you might acquire initially:

- A Recreational Permit. This entitles you to fly most Canadian-registered, single-engine aircraft during the day anywhere within Canada, carrying at most one passenger and staying clear of cloud.

- A Private Pilot Licence. This entitles you to fly most Canadian-registered, single-engine aircraft during the day almost anywhere in the world with as many passengers as the aircraft can carry, but staying clear of cloud.

Neither the Recreational Permit nor the Private Pilot Licence allows you to charge passengers for their trip.

Some students train directly for the Private Pilot Licence, others take the flight test for the Recreational Permit on their way to the Private Pilot Licence and others stick with the Recreational Permit.

Once you have a Private Pilot Licence, there are many more permits and licences that you can acquire.

What will I actually do once I have my licence?

That's limited only by your imagination. Some people use the aircraft as they would a car to explore other towns and areas: from Ottawa I travel regularly into Toronto, Montreal, Quebec City and down into the USA, just for the fun of exploring those places. We have many visitors from Europe, particularly in the summer, and a flight around the city is a great way to show them the area. Other people seem to enjoy tinkering with their aircraft more than flying them. Some people fly unusual aircraft, perhaps "home-builts" or old war planes. During the summer there is always a nearby fly-in event, where you can meet other pilots, look over their aircraft and engage in "hanger talk." Another possibility is to combine flying with other hobbies, photography for example. Taking photographs from the air literally gives a new dimension to the activity.

How old/young do I have to be?

There is no upper age limit; quite frequently there are stories in the aviation magazines of a pilot getting a licence when over 70. There is, however, a lower limit. You need to be 14 before you can fly an aircraft solo, at least 16 before you can get a Recreational Permit and at least 17 before you can obtain a Private Pilot Licence.

Will I have to speak French to fly in Quebec or English to fly in Ontario?

Air Traffic Controllers and Flight Service Station personnel in the Montreal Flight Information Region (FIR), effectively covering Quebec Province, are all bi-lingual and will talk to pilots in French or English, but pilots need only speak in one language. On a couple of occasions, though, I've had problems arriving at airfields in Quebec where I've been the only English speaker on the radio. I felt uncomfortable being unsure of the position of the other aircraft and having the other pilots unsure of mine but, legally, there is no requirement to speak or understand French.

Outside the Montreal Flight Information Region controllers speak only English and pilots must make all of their broadcasts in English. Remember that the messages exchanged between an aircraft and Air Traffic Control are very limited and very formalized. Only a limited vocabulary – and no grammar – is required.

Can I fly in the winter?

I can only speak for the Ottawa area. Here winter flying can be a pleasure while you are airborne. There are fewer thermals (columns of rising air) which makes rides smoother and the thicker air allows engines to achieve more power and helps the aircraft climb more quickly. The problem with winter flying concerns wing-covers, used to keep snow and ice from the wings while the aircraft is parked. Removing and replacing these with the wind howling and a temperature of -20°C lacks some of the charm of strolling to the aircraft in shirt-sleeves in mid-July. Engines also need to be pre-heated when the temperature is low and this can add a cold half-hour to the beginning of any flight.

What will I have to do to fly into an airport? Do I have to book ahead? Do I have to talk to Air Traffic Control?

Transport Canada publishes a thick book every 2 months called the Canada Flight Supplement (CFS).[1] This contains details of all the airports in Canada: their runways, restaurants, radio frequencies, etc. Having found the details of the airport to which you'd like to fly, you make a free telephone call to a Flight Service Station (FSS) to check that the airport is not temporarily closed and then, with the exception of a very few large airports, you simply "turn up." Read "A Sample Flight" to see how a real flight happens.

Will I have to fly where I'm told?

No. With a basic Private Pilot Licence or Recreational Permit you will be flying under what are known as Visual Flight Rules (VFR) and, except for a few restricted areas and some zones around large airports where you have to ask permission to enter, you are allowed to fly wherever you wish and at whatever height you wish (within reason).

How high will I fly?

Most recreational flying takes place below 6500 feet above sea level (except in the mountains where the ground may be higher than that). Most training aircraft have a ceiling (maximum altitude) of about 10 000 feet, but in most you would have to be very patient to reach that height. If you fancy flying very high, then consider gliders rather than powered aircraft; since they have no engine gasping for air and are equipped with oxygen for the pilot, flights over 20 000 feet are common. The Canadian glider altitude record stands currently at 34 400 feet.

Will I have to buy an aircraft when I've finished training?

Most recreational pilots don't – they rent or part-own. Renting is actually the most economical way of flying unless you fly a lot (say, more than 150 hours per year). It is, however, inconvenient as the aircraft has to be returned by a certain time and a lot of the pleasure of flying consists of taking off in the early morning, flying to a remote airport and leaving the aircraft while you explore on foot or by rented car. Also, most clubs renting aircraft will require you to pay for a minimum number of hours (typically 3) each day.

Many pilots therefore form syndicates and own an aircraft jointly with other pilots, reducing the cost but keeping the flexibility of leaving the aircraft on the ground at a remote airfield without incurring rental fees.

Will I have to do maintenance work on my aircraft?

No. During the inspection before each flight there are some basic mechanical checks that you will perform (checking the oil level, checking the correct operation of the flight controls, etc.), but real maintenance is normally left to a professional Aircraft Maintenance Engineer (AME). I say "normally" because owners of home-built aircraft are allowed to do their own maintenance, and there is legislation before Parliament which, if passed, would allow owners of some professionally-built aircraft to carry out their own maintenance. The aircraft so maintained would then fly under a special Certificate of Airworthiness and a notice would have to be displayed in the aircraft stating *"This aircraft does not comply with international recognized standards of airworthiness."* Nor with internationally recognized standards of English grammar.

What about Ultralights and Gliders?

Some years ago ultralights (aircraft having a takeoff weight less than 1200 lbs., about 550 kg) had a reputation for being less reliable than "conventional" aircraft. This certainly isn't true today and the number of makes of ultralight aircraft is increasing almost daily. At the moment ultralight pilots may not carry passengers, but regulations are changing to make this possible. Much as with the Recreational Permit, in return for giving up some flexibility (flying in cloud, flying at night and flying to destinations outside Canada), the student ultralight pilot gets a licence more quickly and more cheaply.

Gliders (also known as sailplanes) are my first love. I learned to fly in gliders in the Welsh Mountains and still feel that it is a truer form of flying. There must be very few glider pilots who have not, on occasion, circled *silently* in a thermal with a hawk or eagle – an overwhelming experience. Without an engine, glider flights can be much longer than those of a power aircraft (a typical training aircraft will only have fuel for a 3 or 4 hour flight, whereas glider flights can last all day; the Canadian distance record for a pre-declared flight stands at just over 1000 km). A glider can fly higher and, of course, is silent. The pilot really is part of the aircraft rather than simply "sitting inside it." Having waxed lyrical about gliding, I must confess that the rest of this book is about power flying, but I refer any reader interested in gliding to Ken Stewart's book[2] for more details.

If you gain your Private Pilot Licence in a conventionally-powered aircraft, then this also authorizes you to fly ultralights, although not gliders.

The Canadian Owners and Pilots Association issues a very useful booklet[3] each year which contains, amongst other information, lists of flying schools which support ultralights and gliders. This publication is available at most bookstores.

Is flying dangerous?

It's definitely more dangerous than lying in bed. I canvassed some potential pilots for their worst fears and collected the following:

🐾 *wings being damaged and falling off.* Aircraft are actually extremely strong and the only accident reports I could find where an aircraft's structure physically failed in normal (non-aerobatic) flight was when one was stupidly flown into a thunderstorm. Aircraft are designed to behave in such a way as to right themselves before damage occurs. Here is an (abbreviated) account of a structural failure in flight:

> *The right wing separated due to over-load as the non-instrument-rated pilot attempted to manoeuver the airplane under a line of convective activity [i.e., thunder clouds] on his route of flight . . . Prior to departure the pilot received weather briefings that included thunderstorm and rainshower activity with VFR flight not recommended.*

🐾 *becoming lost and running out of fuel.* An unscientific poll of inexperienced pilots indicates that their main fear is getting lost and either blundering into controlled airspace or running out of fuel while trying to find the way home. Like most pilots I have had my share of being lost and, frankly, it is disconcerting. There are, however, numerous techniques to find your position. The first is calm map reading – spotting distinctive lakes or hydro-lines and finding these on the map. If this fails then you can try the various radio navigation devices (VORs and NDBs) in the area and get a bearing to or from these. If that fails and you have a GPS, your problems are solved. If all of these fail then it is time to invoke the three Cs of Climb, Confess and Comply: by *Climbing* you make yourself more visible to ATC's radar and you also get a better view of the landscape for map reading; by *Confessing* you can get help from a controller who should be able to pin-point your position on

radar; then, within reason, you must *Comply* with
the controller's instructions.

&& *having the aircraft catch fire*. Again, this does happen,
but extremely rarely. Fires that do occur tend to
originate in the electrical system and, since that system is not required to keep the engine running, you
will be taught to turn off the master electrical switch
as soon as you smell smoke. This silences the radio
(and a hand-held radio can be useful on such an
occasion), but in no way impedes the way in which
the engine runs or the aircraft flies.

&& *being sucked into a thunderstorm*. Thunderstorms are
dangerous. Air is sucked into a thunderstorm and
descends around the outside. Air sinking at 6000
feet per minute has been observed in a large thunderstorm and very few aircraft could climb through
that. A thunderstorm also brings wind-shear – sudden changes in the direction of the wind – and
severe turbulence. As you will not be flying in
cloud, it is normally possible to see thunderstorms
while you are still a long way off and give them a
wide (20 mile) berth.

&& *running into another aircraft*. Mid-air collision is a
genuine danger, particularly when flying near an
airport where all aircraft follow the same path. To
avoid aircraft hitting each other when *en route*, pilots
select heights depending on their direction of flight.
Thus, a pilot flying westwards would fly at 4500,
6500 or 8500 feet and a pilot flying eastwards would
fly at 3500, 5500 or 7500 feet. This does not totally
prevent collisions, but it certainly reduces the risk. It
is ultimately the pilot's responsibility to keep a lookout for other aircraft and to avoid them.

&& *meeting severe turbulence*. Turbulence can be disconcerting, particularly in a small aircraft. It occurs
when air masses moving at different speeds meet:

for example, hot air rising in summer from a paved road, air flowing out of a thunderstorm or vortices left behind by the wing-tips of a fast-moving aircraft. The first of these, the "thermal" rising in summer, is by far the most common. It can make flight uncomfortable, but often the effect of the turbulence can be reduced by flying higher; remember that what pilots of powered aircraft call "turbulence" and avoid, glider pilots call "lift" and seek out. There is, by the way, no such thing as the *air pockets* so beloved of the news media.

✣ *having the aircraft "stop flying."* This is perhaps the most interesting of the fears I've listed here and certainly the most difficult for pilots to understand. It is, however, very prevalent. Many people believe that the engine somehow drags the aircraft into the sky and, should the engine stop, the aircraft will plummet. This is not the case. The engine simply pulls the aircraft along and the air flowing over the wings causes it to fly. This means that, even with a stopped engine, a light aircraft is still a (fairly poor) glider; it doesn't drop like a brick. A typical light aircraft, such as a Cessna 172M, will glide about 8 miles if the engine stops when you are at 6000 feet, allowing you to find a suitable field or road (or even airport). It is salutary to note that a reasonable glider could glide over 40 miles from the same height. The engines in light aircraft are checked every 100 hours or annually and are much less complex than car engines. They have two spark plugs in each cylinder, each driven from a separate magneto, so there is no reliance on a battery except for starting. I don't know when your car engine last stopped of its own accord, but I have had only one complete car engine failure in 25 years of driving and that was caused by a battery problem. Nor do I have my car engine overhauled every 100 hours.

Mechanical failures do occur and engines do stop very occasionally. As part of the primary training, you will be taught to handle the situation and glide to the ground.

✖ *feeling claustrophobic in the "tiny" aircraft.* Most small aircraft have excellent all-round visibility which helps to reduce this feeling and remember that, unlike flying in a commercial airliner, you will be able to see forward. The harnesses which you will use normally include both lap and shoulder straps and have given some of my passengers the feeling of being trapped, but they should be viewed as also giving security.

In summary, none of the fears listed above is to be dismissed lightly, but the risk associated with each is very small. In fact, to judge from the accident reports, the major cause of serious injury in light aircraft seems to be new pilots showing off to their friends and flying lower than is wise or trying to do "tricks." My sympathy for such pilots is strictly limited.

What about my fear of heights?

It is strange, but I have taken many people flying who were afraid to stand at the top of a tall building and look down. None of them has exhibited any fear while flying a mile high in the air and looking down.

How much will it cost and how long will it take?

This is difficult to assess because, to some extent, it depends on how quickly you learn. If you are young, keen and have good hand-eye co-ordination, then your flying time is likely to be less than for an older student with no experience of computer games. Another factor which affects the learning time (and therefore the cost) is how often you take lessons. The 55 hours or so of flight training that you are likely to need can all be flown in a few weeks of intense training and this is probably the least-cost way to a licence. For recreational pilots, however, a large part of the fun is the social side and spreading the course out over several months, flying at weekends and taking the time to chat with the old hands probably makes you a better pilot, but at a slightly higher cost.

Tables 1 and 2 each have two columns, one for the absolute legal minimum and one for more realistic minimum times and costs. The costs have been based on a basic two-seater trainer like a Cessna 150 and it is assumed that you will be flying at least once and preferably twice a week – anything less frequent and you will need more hours. To be realistic, add a further 15% to the totals in tables and for small items. Remember that these costs will be spread out over the course of your training and not be paid in one sum. If you fly once or twice a week, then you will probably take 6 or 7 months to get to the Private Pilot Licence and 4 to 5 months to get to the Recreational Permit.

Table 1: The Cost of a Private Pilot Licence

Item	Legal Minimum	Practical Minimum
Medical	$150	$150
Aircraft rental	45 hrs: $3000	55 hrs: $3500
Instructor	17 hrs: $680	30 hrs: $1200
Ground School Tuition	40 hrs: $200	60 hrs: $200
Ground School Books, etc.	$250	$250
Flight Test	$250	$250
Examination Fee	$120	$120
TOTAL	$4650 (say $5000)	$5670 (say $6000)

Table 2: The Cost of a Recreational Permit

Item	Legal Minimum	Practical Minimum
Medical	$150	$150
Aircraft rental	25 hrs: $1600	35 hrs: $2200
Instructor	15 hrs: $600	25 hrs: $1000
Flight Test Fees	$250	$250
Examination Fee	$120	$120
TOTAL	$2720 (say $3000)	$3720 (say $4000)

A mature person coming to flying in mid-life and flying at most once each week normally takes longer to reach the Flight Test standard. An average of about 70 hours flying could be expected for the Private Pilot Licence and 50 hours for the Recreational Permit. Transport Canada monitors the pass rate of pupils from each instructor and failures count against the instructor's record, so your instructor won't submit you for the formal flight test until you are ready. The average number of flying hours that students have before taking their Flight Test has increased slowly over the years, possibly because instructors are "over-training" to ensure that their pass rate remains high.

Of course, you can spend as much as you like on accessories: perhaps your own headset (I always felt that using club headsets was slightly unhygienic) for about $150, perhaps additional books or computer courses to augment the ground school course. The best investment, in my experience, has been a hand-held radio and VOR receiver. Other useful accessories include a good pair of sun-glasses, a cushion (if you're short), a flight bag to contain all your maps, logs, etc. and a knee-board.

There is fashion in knee-boards! These are useful devices which strap to your thigh to give you a surface for writing notes as you fly along. The more sophisticated makes have lights, pencil holders and other paraphernalia which get in the way. There was a review of the various commercially-available types in the November 1997 edition of the magazine *IFR*[4] which concluded that spending $5 at your local stationery store was probably better than spending $60 with an aviation supplier.

Remember that costs don't end when you have your licence. You will want to continue flying and will have to rent or buy an aircraft. These costs are, however, more controllable.

Will I need to buy special clothes?

No. It has been said that, as a group and speaking in general, recreational pilots are not among the best-dressed members of society. Once in the air, the ventilation in a light aircraft is much like that in a car: there are air vents for the summer and a heater working off the heat from the engine in the winter.

Training

Licences

You could probably spend the rest of your life studying for licences, ratings and permits of various types. As a first step, you will earn a Recreational Permit or a Private Pilot Licence. The Recreational Permit is easier to get, but doesn't allow you to do as much as the Private Pilot Licence. With a Recreational Permit you may only carry one passenger, fly during the day and only within Canada. As many aircraft are two-seaters, summer days are long and Canada is a large place, these restrictions are not particularly onerous, but most pilots do eventually work to obtain their Private Pilot Licence.

The steps to a Private Pilot Licence and Recreational Permit are basically the same and are shown in the diagram below. Once you have one of these licences, you will be allowed to fly in what are known as Visual Meteorological Conditions (VMC) in accordance with the Visual Flight Rules (VFR). Flying VFR gives you freedom

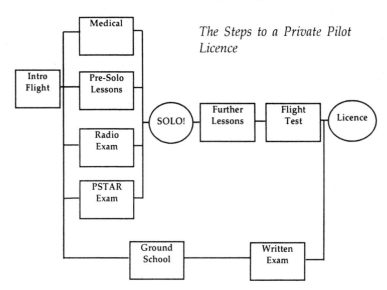

The Steps to a Private Pilot Licence

and responsibility. By remaining clear of cloud and keeping the ground in sight, you can effectively fly anywhere in Canada by any route and at any altitude. Flying VFR has its responsibilities, as no controller on the ground is looking after you and ensuring that you're staying clear of other aircraft.

When the weather deteriorates and you cannot stay clear of cloud or cannot keep the ground in sight, then as a VFR pilot you are stuck, one hopes on the ground rather than in the air. With extra training, you may fly in Instrument Meteorological Conditions (IMC) in accordance with Instrument Flight Rules (IFR), without being able to see the ground. As you can't see other aircraft when flying in IMC, controllers on the ground take the responsibility of keeping you clear of other IFR aircraft; in return you lose the freedom of flying by whatever route you choose.

There is a compromise rating that a VFR pilot can obtain without undergoing the full additional training for the IFR rating: VFR over-the-top (OTT). This rating allows you to fly over solid cloud as long as the aircraft is fitted with certain equipment and as long as the weather forecast for your destination indicates that there will be breaks in the cloud around your expected arrival time. This rating does not allow you to fly through cloud: simply to climb through a gap in the clouds, fly above cloud or between two cloud layers and then descend through a gap. I must say that I doubt the wisdom of VFR OTT. The obvious question is, "what happens when the forecast was wrong and the destination airport is under a solid cloud layer?" In these conditions a pilot with a full IFR rating will have been trained to follow radio signals from the airport down to within 200 feet of the ground, but a VFR OTT pilot is, frankly, in trouble.

A few years ago, before I was allowed to fly IFR, my wife and I went on holiday to New Brunswick, intending to take two days flying from Ottawa, via Quebec City, to

Grand Manan island in the Bay of Fundy. We made good progress on the first day and reached Grand Falls, New Brunswick. Next morning we awoke to find the cloud overcast at about 1000 feet. The Flight Service Station that I rang to get the weather forecast anticipated that it would stay that way for days. Unable to take off, we quickly exhausted the tourist possibilities of Grand Falls on a rainy day and had to rent a car to continue our trip. Had I had an Instrument Rating, we could have taken off through the cloud and been in the sunshine within a few minutes. The Instrument Rating is therefore a very useful add-on rating for a private pilot, as the training also improves your VFR flying and gives you more confidence when talking to ATC.

The major differences between the training for the Recreational Permit and the full Private Pilot Licence are that the Recreational Permit requires no formal Ground School and fewer aerial manoeuvres. When the Recreational Permit was first introduced, there was confusion about whether someone wanting a Recreational Permit on their way to a Private Pilot Licence had to take two separate written examinations; there are now numerous precedents for taking only the (more difficult) Private Pilot examination before getting a Recreational Permit.

Of the steps in getting a licence, perhaps the one which trips up most students is getting the aviation medical out of the way. You cannot fly solo until you have a medical certificate and obtaining a certificate can take longer than you imagine: allow a week to get an appointment with an aviation medical examiner, assume that he or she sends your certificate off to Transport Canada within a couple of days and then allow 4 more days in the mail before it arrives. Two weeks have more or less gone already. I have known medicals to take up to 3 weeks to get back from Transport Canada (in fact, I've known them to be lost altogether). This means that it could take 5 weeks or more before you have the medical certificate you need to go solo. Typically you could expect to solo after 10 to 15 hours of tuition, so you could well be ready before your medical is. Once you have the class 3 medical for the Private Pilot Licence, it is valid for two years if you are younger than 40, or for one year if you are older.

The Recreational Permit, although easier and quicker to get, is something of a dead end. The only additional rating that you can add to it is that for flying floatplanes, allowing you to land and take off from the lakes and rivers with which Canada abounds.

Students with the Private Pilot Licence have more options and those with normal color vision typically take the Night Rating, which enables them to fly after dark, and then stop formal training. Beyond this are the Commercial Licence, which enables you to fly professionally, and the Instrument Rating described above. These two additional steps can be taken in either order. A Commercial Licence is clearly the next stepping stone for students intending to become professional pilots. This licence involves more Ground School, a long cross-country and a virtual repeat of the Private Pilot flight test, but with a higher pass-mark.

Flight Training

Learning to fly comes in two parts: the practical (flying) and the theoretical (Ground School). This section and the next deal with these two topics.

One question many students ask is whether they should take Ground School before or after starting their actual flying. My advice is to try to time the flight training to start a couple of weeks before the Ground School. This way you will come to the Ground School with some basic understanding of the feel of the aircraft and the classes won't be totally theoretical. In Ground School, for example, you'll learn that 100LL fuel is colored blue. If you've refuelled your training aircraft a few times, then this is something you won't have to learn – you will have seen it.

Of course, not all ground training takes place in Ground School. Each flying lesson typically starts and ends with a discussion with your instructor on the ground, briefing you for the lesson and debriefing you afterwards. As you progress through your training, the format will change, with the amount of ground briefing decreasing and the flight time increasing. This is particularly true once you are cleared to fly solo – you'll then have one solo flight for every couple of dual flights to allow you to practise what you've learned.

Before you start your training, you must choose a flying school and an instructor. If you have several flying schools within reach, then you might like to shop around, but since all clubs monitor the prices charged at the others, you're unlikely to find a significant saving at one rather than another. I suggest you visit the clubs around lunch-time on a sunny weekend day and see which has the social atmosphere that you'd like to be part of: are pilots sitting around the barbecue chatting with the instructors and students, or is the atmosphere more formal? There are two other differentiators you might like to consider: type of airfield and type of aircraft.

Some flying schools are based at controlled airports (airports with control towers). They argue that their pupils learn to fly in a professional environment and never have any nervousness in approaching and landing at a large airport. They don't mention the hesitancy their pupils have approaching an uncontrolled airport for the first time, finding themselves responsible for selecting a runway and clearing themselves to land.

Flying schools at uncontrolled airports, on the other hand, stress the time they save the students: no waiting at the end of a runway with the engine running (and the student paying) while a commercial flight departs. In fact, I feel that the differences are probably minimal. I learned at an uncontrolled airport and was certainly uncomfortable landing at my first few controlled airports, Ottawa's MacDonald-Cartier and Quebec City's Jean Lesage International, but the feeling soon wore off.

You might also like to consider the type of aircraft used for training. Until very recently there was little choice – Piper or Cessna aircraft of 1960s and 1970s vintage. Recently a new wave of aircraft has come onto the scene, including Diamond's Katana. These new aircraft are sleeker, more comfortable and generally better equipped than the somewhat dated Pipers and Cessnas. Again, the difference is probably not enough to worry about: for me conversion from a Cessna 172 to a Katana took only two short check-out flights. Converting the other way may take slightly longer.

Having found your club, you will then have to find an instructor. You will probably take pot luck for your first lesson, but don't be afraid to change instructors if you don't feel that you're getting along together or you're not comfortable with the instructor's style. Unfortunately, most instructors are not career teachers – they are often young commercial pilots building hours before getting a job with an airline. This, coupled with poor pay, means that their eyes are always on the job market and they eventually depart, often giving little notice. It is therefore wise to fly with at least two different instructors on a regular basis, if only to compare what they tell you. I have had instructors who never stopped talking long enough for me to think and others who rarely said a word and seemed to enjoy just staring out of the window. Keep searching until you find one who matches your learning style.

Your instructor will keep a record of your flying hours, with comments on how the lessons went; this will be needed when you take your test flight, so make sure that it gets completed accurately. You will also keep a record of your flying hours in your own log book. One criticism that I have of almost all commercially available log books is that they have very little space to record the details of the flight – they contain instead plenty of columns for recording things like the number of hours flown in single-seater biplanes after 6 o'clock in the evening. Before buying a log book, browse around and, if it suits you better, get one with fewer flights per page but with more room to record your impressions, lessons learned, etc. Remember that, although the law requires you to keep this log, it is *your* book, through which you'll probably want to browse in later years. A single line saying "CYRO to CYSH" will bring back few memories, whereas "Rockcliffe to Smiths Falls with Fred: photographed his cottage from above the river" may.

There are several manoeuvres that you will have to learn so that you can satisfy the examiner during the Flight Test and these are described below. *The Flight Training Manual* from Transport Canada has a full description of each of these exercises.

Taxiing, Taking off and Landing

Aircraft, like most birds, are adapted for flight rather than moving around on the ground and taxiing can be surprisingly difficult, particularly in aircraft such as the Katana, which does not have nose-wheel steering. Normally, steering on the ground is accomplished with a combination of differential braking and use of the nose-wheel, all performed with the feet. I always try to remember to brief new passengers on the fact that, while on the ground, I'll be steering with my feet, otherwise I find them puzzled by the aircraft wandering around the airport while my hands are resting idly on a stationary control column. Another consideration when taxiing is the wind strength and direction. On occasion pilots have landed successfully in a nasty cross-wind only to be blown over when taxiing.

Taking off cleanly in an aircraft is harder than it looks. Many pilots simply tear down the runway and yank the aircraft into the air. This can be effective (unless attempted at too low an airspeed), but is inelegant and unrewarding. In a nasty cross-wind it may be necessary to get more speed and then get the aircraft airborne quickly to avoid drifting sideways, but normally a takeoff should be a co-operative venture between an aircraft that wants to fly and a pilot who allows it to.

Landing is probably the most exciting and difficult part of flight training. Most training is carried out sufficiently high above the ground for you to have time to get out of any mess you get into but, obviously, landing takes place close to the ground. When landing, you will also be travelling relatively slowly and so there is less room for error. Generally height and speed are what keep an aircraft safe: if you do something silly at height then you can recover before you reach the ground; if you are low and fast then you can climb and convert the speed into height. If you are slow and low, then any problem can leave you with few options.

Any pilot who says that all his or her landings are greasers either has low standards or a long nose. My landings tend to go in phases: a bunch of really good ones followed, probably when I get too relaxed, with a bunch of poor ones.

The wind plays a surprisingly large part in landings. Aircraft generally take-off and land into the wind. Since runways are fixed to the ground and the winds are not, times arise when the wind is blowing across rather than down the runway. In these cross-wind conditions, you will be taught to move the control column into wind and then apply opposite rudder to keep the aircraft moving directly towards the runway, albeit with one side of the aircraft lower than the other. This needs a sensitive touch on the pedals and control column, but is very rewarding when flown well.

For the flight test you will be asked to demonstrate a normal takeoff and landing, and the type of takeoff and landing that you would use from a short or soft field. Since fields may be both short *and* soft, I used to ask my instructors how one combined these techniques, but never got a clear answer.

It will probably be after a series of circuits consisting of taking off, flying back to the landing end of the runway and landing that your instructor, choosing a day with light winds and good visibility, will ask you to taxi back to the club-house and allow him to get out. He will then send you once more around on your own, your first solo and a flight which you will never forget.

My first solo took place in a glider in the Mid-Wales mountains and was even less expected because, following a glider landing, everyone has to help to push it back to the launch point. There is always a queue of people waiting to use the training gliders and, following an hour's flight with my instructor, Doc Saundby, we got out and pushed the glider back. I was collecting up my things when he said, "I think you ought to go up again, Chris." I was pleased but surprised that I was being allowed to jump the queue and climbed back in, half observing Doc moving around to the back seat. He secured the seat belt in the back and walked away and it was clear that this was to be a solo. He told me to be away for 30 minutes at most, reminded me that the glider would be lighter and therefore take-off earlier without him in the back and, by the time I understood what was happening, the tug aircraft was already approaching with the tow rope and I went into automatic, carrying out the pre-flight checks (CB-SIFT-CB: Controls free and correct, Ballast correct, Straps done up, Instruments set, Flaps not fitted, Trim correct, Canopy down and locked and Air Brakes away), signaling for the tow rope to be attached and for the tug plane to start taking up the slack before the enormity of what I was doing hit me. In the event, I flew for only 19 minutes, giving up and running for home as soon as I hit a patch of sinking air, but I lived on the experience for weeks.

One spin-off from your first solo is a year's free membership in COPA, the Canadian Owners' and Pilots' Association. This organization issues a monthly newspaper which is, of necessity, somewhat worthy and dull. COPA fights for the rights of General Aviation (fighting the closure of runways, introduction of landing fees and taxes on aircraft ownership, etc.) and this is not generally the stuff of gripping journalism. The magazine admittedly does contain a lot of useful information, normally including the description of a flight that some member has undertaken to a remote corner of Canada.

Stalls and Spins

Landings are difficult and, when done well, rewarding, but spins are pure fun. I learned to do them first in gliders where they are much more dramatic. Stalls and spins in powered aircraft are largely non-events, but must be practised.

Stalls are probably the manoeuver most misunderstood by non-pilots. A car "stalls" when its engine stops. An aircraft's stalling has nothing to do with the engine; it can occur with the engine at full power or with the engine switched off and even in a glider which has no engine at all. If you are flying along and pull back on the control column, then the nose will lift and the aircraft will try to climb. If you don't add power, then the aircraft will fly more slowly. If you continue to pull the nose up, then the wing will make an increasingly large angle with the air flow. Eventually the air flow will no longer follow the surface of the wing. You will feel this as a vibration and, when it occurs, the wing stops giving lift and, in most training aircraft, the aircraft's nose drops gently and the air starts to flow across the wing again. Nothing to get excited about in the air, but very difficult to explain in Ground School to a student who hasn't experienced it.

A spin occurs when only one wing stalls. The aircraft tumbles through the air, which can be disconcerting, but recovery is easy and quick.

In the flight test you will be required to demonstrate stalls and during your training you will experience spins.

Flying has a lot to do with checklists and, since stalls and spins are considered "aerobatic" (although not by aerobatic pilots), you will be taught another checklist to go through before you attempt them: HAASEL. These letters stand for:

⊠ Height: do you have enough of it?

⊠ Airframe: is it rated for this exercise?

⊠ Area: are you over a nice open, rural area?

⊠ Security: are you strapped in and is everything secure in the back?

⊠ Engine: is the carburetor heat on, etc.?

⊠ Lookout: is there another aircraft about, particularly beneath you?

Steep Turns

An aircraft turns by banking (for a highly emotional but completely accurate explanation of banking – the only one in aviation literature – see the glossary entry) into the direction of the turn and the steeper the angle of bank or the slower the aircraft is moving, the tighter the turn. Holding the aircraft precisely at a given angle of bank while staying at the same altitude is a delicate exercise, since the aircraft will try to descend as the bank increases. The steep turn exercise allows you to demonstrate mastery of the aircraft when turning through 360° in a 45° bank.

There is a misunderstanding about this exercise. Many instructors believe that you have made a successful steep turn if, on straightening out, you run into your own wake (the disturbed air behind the aircraft). The wake of an aircraft, however, drops below the aircraft, so if you do run into your own wake you have actually dropped during the turn.

Slipping

It is normally the job of the pilot to ensure that the aircraft is flying cleanly through the air and he or she does this by glancing from time-to-time at one of the least sophisticated but most useful of the instruments on the panel: the turn-and-slip indicator. This is just a ball in a U-tube of liquid (rather like an inverted spirit-level). If the aircraft is flying correctly then the ball sits in the middle of the tube, at its lowest point. Cutting through the air cleanly is even more important in a glider and glider pilots tape a short length of wool onto the cockpit window so that they don't need to look down at the turn-and-slip indicator. If the glider is flying cleanly through the air then the wool streams straight back.

There are times, such as when you need to lose height quickly, when it is useful to fly the aircraft inefficiently through the air. By turning the aircraft partially sideways, the drag (resistance of the air) increases enormously and the aircraft drops rapidly (and inexperienced passengers turn green). This trick, known as slipping or skidding, is achieved by moving the control column in one direction, say to bank the aircraft to the right, and then moving the rudder to the left. The aircraft continues to fly in something approaching a straight line, but with the nose pointing off to the right. In some aircraft which are not fitted with flaps, slipping is the only method for increasing the rate of descent during an approach to land.

Spiral Dive

The spiral dive is another manoeuvre from which you learn to recover. Again, the procedure is not as exciting as it sounds. What happens is that, while turning, the aircraft starts to drop and accelerate. If you do nothing to recover, then the turn will get tighter and tighter and the aircraft will go faster and faster until the inevitable happens.

In the test the examiner will deliberately put the aircraft into a spiral dive and then ask you to recover. My examiner had a little script here: "I am going to take control of the aircraft. If you see me doing anything potentially dangerous then you are to take control back and recover." She then flew around for a few minutes, making left and right turns until one turn started to become a spiral dive.

I must admit to accidentally putting an aircraft into the beginnings of a spiral dive once while I was a solo student. I was flying around the circuit (i.e., taking off, flying back to land and repeating) at Rockcliffe, an uncontrolled airport, and there were a lot of other aircraft arriving and taking off. On one lap, while turning back to the runway, I found that I was close behind another aircraft and decided to fly a circle to allow it to get further ahead of me. I made a radio call to say what I was doing and, while turning around the circle, my attention was outside the cockpit, trying to locate the other aircraft and, when I looked back at the instruments, I found myself dropping and speeding up, the beginning of a spiral dive. However, I had been trained what to do and recovered quickly.

Slow Flight

There is a paradox associated with flying an aircraft slowly. Imagine that you are flying along straight and level at 100 knots with the engine running at 2300 rpm. If you reduce the engine power to, say, 1900 rpm, the aircraft will start to descend. Pull back on the control column to keep the aircraft at the same altitude and it will start to fly along at, perhaps, 70 knots. Reduce the power again to 1500 rpm and again keep the aircraft from sinking by pulling back yet further. The nose goes up even more and the drag caused by flying through the air with the nose pointing upwards like this increases dramatically. To fly even slower while maintaining the same altitude, you have to *add* power, possibly back to 1900 rpm – you add power to fly more slowly.

Flying along at a speed close to the stall speed, with the aircraft's nose held high, is called "slow flight." For the flight test you will have to demonstrate getting into slow flight, performing a simple manoeuvre (such as turning through 360° or climbing 500 feet), and then returning to normal flight.

I found that the trick in slow flight was not to rush it. There is no time limit on the activities during the flight test. Reduce power *and wait for the aircraft to settle to a new speed*. Then, and only then, reduce power further: feel your way into slow flight.

Instrument Flying

During your training you will fly for at least 5 hours "under the hood." There are various types of hood but all are designed to prevent you seeing anything except the instruments; in particular, you can't see out of the window, thus simulating conditions in a cloud.

There are three basic types of hood:

- devices with a band around the head and a drop-down visor like a welder's mask. When coupled with headphones, this type of hood can be very uncomfortable.

- devices called "foggles," similar to a pair of eye glasses with the top half of each lens fogged. I wear glasses anyway and find wearing a second pair on

top, particularly as both have to go under the head-
phone's ear-piece, very uncomfortable.

📇 devices which clip onto the metal brackets of the
headset. These seem the best of a bad job, being
comfortable, even when worn with glasses, and able
to block all peripheral vision of the outside world.
They can also be flipped up and down quickly to
make the transition between simulated cloud and
reality.

You can cheat with any type of hood, since it is very
difficult for the instructor or examiner to determine what
you can and cannot see, but remember who you're cheating: yourself. It's a bit like cheating at solitaire, but possibly with more serious consequences, since this training is
supposed to protect you if you inadvertently fly into a
cloud and need to turn around to get out. This is not as
simple as you would imagine, because your senses can
tell you, for example, that you're climbing when you're
actually dropping.

In the flight test you'll be asked to fly for a couple of
minutes straight and level, then turn 180 degrees and fly
again for a minute or so, all with the hood on. Since learning to do this doesn't normally take 5 hours, your instructor will probably use the excess time to teach you more
sophisticated skills: climbing, descending, navigating to
radio beacons, etc.

If you continue your training past the Private Pilot
Licence to get an Instrument Rating, then you'll have to
fly at least another 35 hours under the hood.

Emergencies

The operating handbook for the aircraft in which you
learn to fly will have lists of emergency procedures. Here,
for example, is the procedure for an "Engine Failure
During Takeoff Run" in a Cessna 172M:

📇 Throttle – idle

- Brakes – apply
- Wing Flaps – retract
- Mixture – idle cut-off
- Ignition Switch – off

Now, if your engine fails during the take-off roll, and you lean over to pick up the operating handbook, find the correct page and read through this list, it is likely that the aircraft will have stopped before you find your place. You will therefore have to commit these lists to memory. I have a terrible memory and my wife even suggested setting the lists to music to get them into my head: should I apply brakes *before* or *after* retracting the wing flaps? Does it matter?

This is one topic where sitting by yourself in the aircraft, with the engine turned off, is useful. Find a training aircraft that's not in use, sit in it and go through the emergency procedures touching each control so that it is second nature. It really does help and, since the engine isn't switched on, it doesn't cost anything either. During World War 2, trainee pilots were required to pass a test whereby they had to identify and touch every control in the aircraft on demand while blindfolded. This is a useful (and free) exercise: once when flying in a new type of aircraft I accidentally pulled the Mixture Control (used to stop the engine) instead of the throttle.

During your flight test you will be asked about a couple of emergencies and at least one, the forced landing, will have to be demonstrated. At some time in the flight the examiner will pull the throttle to idle (but not switch the engine off) and say that you have had an engine failure. You will pretend to check the engine, fail to find the reason for the failure, pretend to make a MAYDAY call, select a field and line up to land in it. Just before landing the examiner will take pity on you and allow you to apply power again.

I thought that my examiner was a bit sneaky on this point; I was just recovering from the spiral dive and congratulating myself and relaxing when she suddenly pulled the power and announced the (simulated) emergency. Before getting frightened about forced landings, remember that all glider landings are forced landings and glider pilots don't make a fuss (much).

Engine Failures

Although genuine engine failures are very rare, they do occur and a pilot does need to be aware of the threat. There are actually two main causes of engine stopping: lack of fuel and carburetor icing. I have little sympathy for pilots who run out of fuel, since we know how much fuel our aircraft burns per hour and we know (or should know) how much fuel is in the tank when we take off. Unless one accidentally leaves a fuel cap off, the time of fuel exhaustion can be calculated quite accurately. Here's a typical accident report (slightly edited) regarding fuel exhaustion:

A Piper PA-24-250 collided with terrain following an engine power loss. The private pilot had minor injuries. The aircraft was substantially damaged.

The pilot reported that he landed the day before the accident with the left fuel tank selected, which was the fuller tank. At the time, the left tank indicated half full. On the morning of the accident flight, he pre-flighted the airplane [i.e., <u>checked the aircraft before flying it</u>], and both tanks indicated half full on the gauges. He did not perform a visual inspection of either tank prior to the accident flight. During the five minute flight, he retarded the throttle for the descent. When he added power, there was no response to throttle inputs. He set up for a forced landing in a cotton field. During the approach to the cotton field, he turned to align the airplane with the parallel rows of cotton. The aircraft stalled about 10 feet above the ground, and "nosed in."

An inspector visited the accident site and inspected the wreckage. He reported that the aircraft came to rest in a flat, open field. The area around the aircraft was absent of any ground scars, and there was evidence that the aircraft had impacted the ground in a steep, nose low attitude. The right wing fuel tank was empty of fuel, as was the fuel sump. The fuel tank selector valve was found in the right tank position.

There are a few points to note in this report:

- ✂ the pilot's injuries were only minor. This is often the case in light aircraft accidents since light aircraft tend to fly quite slowly and, in many, the pilot is well protected.

- ✂ the pilot did not look into the fuel tanks during his pre-flight inspection, but relied on the fuel gauges. Fuel gauges are notoriously inaccurate.

- ✂ no flight is too short for an accident to occur.

- ✂ contrary to popular belief, the expression "the aircraft stalled" does not refer to the engine stopping: see page 36 for details of stalling.

The other major cause of engine stopping is carburetor icing, which can occur when the humidity and temperature are conducive, and this is avoided by pulling a knob in the cabin to force hot air through the carburetor every 15 minutes or so. Some pilots carry a timer to remind them of the need to apply carburetor heat. Carburetor icing also occurs in cars, but they have automatic systems to melt it – something that could be introduced into aircraft, but which has been resisted because it results in a loss of power.

Navigation

For me, navigation and popping out of a cloud, lined up for a runway, are what make flying fun. With the advent of the Global Positioning System (GPS), any pilot, armed with a $500 hand-held GPS receiver, can tell the aircraft's position to within 30m or so at any time. Some pilots would not dream of taking off without their GPS and simply "follow the needle" to their destination.

This is certainly one way to fly but, for me, marking up the map, spotting way-points and using the E6B slide rule (see right side of photograph) to deduce ground speeds and timings is a lot more fun. Spotting way-points on the ground is also an activity which passengers seem to enjoy and it keeps them interested on a long flight. I have recently discovered the delights of transparent yellow adhesive tape available from pilot equipment shops. This can be laid across a map without obscuring the information underneath, will take ink for marking waypoints and, when the trip is over, will lift off without damaging or marking the map.

However much innocent pleasure we get from marking up maps, we would be foolish to ignore the electronic devices. Recently I was ferrying a Cessna 172 from Ottawa to Peterborough, Ontario, to have new navigation equipment installed. The old equipment already having been removed, the aircraft had no navigation devices at all beyond the magnetic compass. The weather forecast was favorable, predicting 25 mile visibility and high cloud, but totally wrong. As I got within 30 miles of Peterborough, the cloud started to descend and I was eventually forced down to about 1600 feet (about 1000 feet above ground). As conditions deteriorated, I reached for my hand-held GPS in my flight bag, only to find that I had foolishly forgotten to pack it. I then remembered my hand-held radio, which I always carry, and which has a rudimentary VOR navigation receiver.

A VOR is like a lighthouse for aircraft: it transmits a radio signal to allow an aircraft to determine the direction to the transmitter (see photograph). Until the advent of GPS, almost all radio navigation was performed by flying along airways from VOR to VOR. Before VORs were introduced, there were Non-Directional Beacons (NDBs). An NDB is more primitive than a VOR and, as its name implies, transmits freely in all directions. A receiver in the aircraft, called an Automatic Direction Finder (ADF), can pick up the signal and point a needle towards the transmitter. Actually, any AM radio station can act as an NDB and many pilots tune into AM radio stations, using their ADFs for in-flight entertainment. The Canada Flight Supplement actually gives a list of many AM radio stations across Canada. A disadvantage of the NDB is that

A VOR transmitter, the aircraft's lighthouse. Photo Peter Woolliams.

the needle will also tend to point to thunderstorms, luring the unwitting pilot to destruction.

By using my hand-held VOR receiver I was able to fly directly away from the VOR in a direction that I knew from the map would take me over the town of Peterborough. This I did and, while "temporarily uncertain of my position on the ground," was able to find the airport.

This is the second time that this hand-held radio has proven invaluable to me, the first time being in cloud flying to Montreal's Mirabel airport with my instructor. As we approached Mirabel, I tuned the Instrument Landing System for the approach and then went to tune the radio to Mirabel Tower. The tuning knob broke off. No amount of ingenuity would get it back on and no amount of finger-nail breaking would allow us to tune the radio. My instructor had to plug his head-phones into my hand-held radio and write down for me the clearances that he was receiving: "Cleared for the Approach," "Cleared to Land," "Exit on Taxiway Charlie." I cannot recommend too strongly spending any excess cash after your training on a hand-held radio with navigation features.

During Ground School you will be taught a highly involved way to mark up a map and deduce a plan for your flight. I must admit that nowadays I don't do all that I was taught, but I still draw a line, mark waypoints and tick them off as I spot them from the air.

One question which students often ask during their training is whether the flight-simulator packages available for personal computers are of any use in learning to fly. One area where they are extremely useful is in learning to use the radio navigation aids: the VORs and NDBs. These two devices, and particularly the VOR, can be quite non-intuitive and a few sessions of finding airports using this type of navigation is worth its weight in instructor time. A few months ago I took a young lad, about 13 years old, up in a light aircraft for the first time. He surprised me by asking whether there was a VOR in the neighborhood. I told him the frequency of the local VOR and he then flew me directly to it. Back on the ground I expressed surprise only to learn that he'd been using them on his flight simulator for years. Most instructors will tell you that, apart from navigation exercises, the flight simulators on personal computers are useless or worse than useless, but I'm not sure that this is true. Landing a real aircraft is substantially easier than landing a simulator, but I believe that landing the simulator can be useful in learning to make small movements of the controls. Personally I get a great deal of satisfaction from virtually landing the Lear Jet on the aircraft carrier, something that I'll probably never get the opportunity to do in real life.

When you progress beyond the Private Pilot Licence to the Instrument Rating, you will find that some of your "flying" hours can actually take place in an approved simulator. These approved simulators are substantially more primitive than the ones available on a personal computer but, as long as you are accompanied by an instructor, this time may be logged and counted towards your rating.

You will have to navigate through two long cross-countries (flights to airfields well away from your home base) during your flight training for your Private Pilot Licence, one with an instructor and one supposedly solo. I say "supposedly" because of a loop-hole that has arisen since the introduction of the Recreational Pilot Permit. Many student pilots are now getting a Recreational Permit before their Private Pilot Licence. There is no cross-country requirement for the Recreational Permit (although a pilot may fly from Vancouver to Goose Bay the day after getting a Recreational Permit) and so the pilot's first formal cross-country will be for the Private Pilot Licence. The regulations say that, for this cross-country, the student pilot must be pilot-in-command.

Previously this meant that he or she had to be solo, but now, armed with a Recreational Permit, a student may take a passenger on his or her "solo" cross-country.

The most common mistake made by beginners in navigating is trying to micro-navigate: looking on the ground for everything that's on the map. After a while you will relax, find a lake or other distinctive feature a long way ahead which is on your route and then fly to it, simply enjoying the other scenery passing by underneath. Even ded reckoning (using the E6B to estimate times and distances) is remarkably precise; you can normally fly for 20 minutes and then pass a way-point within 30 seconds of the calculated time.

Although flying by the Visual Flight Rules means that you have to have to be able to see the ground at all times, it obviously does not preclude the use of other navigation devices such as GPS, VORs and NDBs. When flying on instruments in cloud, the ground cannot be seen and all navigation is carried out using GPS, VORs and NDBs.

For the Private Pilot flight test you will be required to plan a cross-country flight, prepare a flight plan and fly enough of the cross-country to convince the examiner that you can find your way without getting unduly lost.

Precautionary Landing

This is an excuse for the instructor or examiner to wax poetic. They normally invent some excuse as to why you need to land soon. Unlike a forced landing, the engine is running but perhaps your passenger has become very ill and needs immediate assistance or perhaps the clouds have been getting lower and lower. Whatever the excuse, you need to find a field, examine it by flying over it a couple of times and then line up to land. Once the examiner sees that you're going to reach the field, he or she will announce that the passenger has had a miraculous recovery or that the clouds have suddenly dissipated and you can overshoot.

A knowledge of agricultural practices in the areas over which you're likely to be flying can make the difference between a successful and unsuccessful precautionary (or forced) landing.

Diversion

This is another excuse for examiner creativity. The story this time is that "the clouds have dropped to 1300 feet and that town down there is *this* one on the map. We need to get to *this* place here and could you please give me an estimate of how long it will take?" Navigation at low level is much harder than when flying high. From height you can see the shapes of the lakes and rivers, from low down you see the next field.

I am ashamed to say that, on my pre-flight test (a sort of mock test with my instructor before taking the real test), I not only flew to the wrong town, I positively identified it (it had a river and railway and was just south of a main road . . . but so was the next town to the west). My problem was the aircraft's Heading Indicator. This is a simple, gyroscopically-driven device which tells you the direction in which you're flying. Because it's driven by a gyroscope, it wanders over time and, about every 15 minutes, you have to reset it using the magnetic compass. By the time I came to fly my diversion, the flight test was an hour or so old and, in my nervousness, I had completely forgotten to reset the Heading Indicator. I estimated a heading from the map and set off flying the wrong heading very accurately. A town hove into view at much the estimated time and I identified it. It's a pity really that, unlike many Ontario towns, it didn't have a water tower with the town's name in large letters. Only when I'd made a complete fool of myself did the instructor remind me to reset the Heading Indicator, now over 20 degrees in error.

By the way, don't belittle town names on tall structures. I was once completely lost during a precision navigation competition (this is a true story!) and had to descend to read a town name on a water tower. I didn't win the navigation competition, but I did find out where I was.

You may ask why, if the Heading Indicator is in need of continual adjustment from the magnetic compass, one doesn't fly using just the compass. This is because, unless you're flying absolutely straight and level at a constant speed, the magnetic compass is even more in error than the Heading Indicator.

Remember to reset the Heading Indicator regularly and you won't have any trouble with the diversion.

Ground Training

However well you fly the aircraft, there are some written examinations that you will have to take, two of them before you are allowed to fly solo (see page 27).

The Radio Examination

The radio examination is the simplest of them all: there is a short booklet, published by Industry Canada and available at any flying club and some good bookstores, called the *Study Guide for the Radiotelephone Operator's Restricted Certificate (Aeronautical)*.[5] The title is the longest part of the document. It describes the phonetic alphabet (how to spell out letters on the radio: ALPHA, BRAVO, CHARLIE, DELTA, ECHO, FOXTROT, GOLF, HOTEL . . . YANKEE, ZULU), the restricted vocabulary used over the radio, how to make an urgent (PAN) or emergency (MAYDAY) call yourself and what to do if you hear someone else making one.

The phonetic alphabet is used when saying the aircraft's call sign and when any single letters need to be said over the radio. A good, but probably apocryphal, tale of a misunderstanding about the phonetic alphabet concerns the inexperienced pilot arriving for the first time at a large airport. These airports broadcast the weather repeatedly on the radio (on a system called the Automatic Terminal Information Service or ATIS) and identify the particular broadcast by a letter (A, B, C, D, etc.) throughout the day. If the broadcast has the code letter H then it will end "inform ATC on initial contact that you have information HOTEL." The scene is now set for the hapless student:

> *Pilot: Ottawa Terminal, this is Cessna 172 FOXTROT PAPA TANGO NOVEMBER, just north of Arnprior at 3000 feet.*
>
> *Ottawa Terminal: PAPA TANGO NOVEMBER, squawk 1234, say your point of departure and intentions.*
>
> *Pilot: PAPA TANGO NOVEMBER is out of Dogsville and we would like to land at Ottawa airport, please.*
>
> *Ottawa Terminal: Roger, PAPA TANGO NOVEMBER, do you have HOTEL?*
>
> *Pilot: Thanks anyway, but we'll be staying with friends.*

It is sad to think that this is an example of pilot humor at its best.

I found the best way to learn the phonetic alphabet was to spell out car licence plates and large words on advertising billboards until I could do it quickly and without thinking.

There are also some special words used over the radio: a real pilot, for example, never says "YES," saying instead "AFFIRMATIVE." This isn't just jargon; it's less easy to misunderstand AFFIRMATIVE when it matters over a poor quality radio channel. These uncommon words are also listed in the *Study Guide* and are chosen to be easily understood even by those with a limited command of English.

You can take the examination at your own flying club and can take it as many times as you like until you pass.

The PSTAR Examination

While the radio examination is designed to ensure that you know enough about radio procedures to fly by yourself, the PSTAR examination is designed to show that you know enough about air law to stay out of trouble once your instructor steps out of the aircraft.

Again this is a multiple-choice examination, but this time, to make things more interesting, you are given the questions beforehand. The examination itself consists of 50 questions taken from about 200 contained in the Aviation Regulation Examination PSTAR document.[6] Your instructor will give you that document and ask you to find the answers in the Canadian Pilot's bible: the A.I.P. Canada.[7] This document, again available from flying clubs and good bookshops, contains extracts from the laws and regulations which pilots must follow. One of the least fun things associated with flying is filing the amendments to the A.I.P., which are issued 4 times annually.

A lot of the A.I.P. is not relevant to recreational pilots (a whole section, for example, deals with flying the Atlantic and much of it deals with instrument flying) but those parts that *are* relevant need to be known and a good way of learning is to look up the answers to the 200 PSTAR questions. This not only prepares you for the 50 questions on the PSTAR, but also for the Air Law part of the Private Pilot Licence written examination.

Again, the PSTAR may be taken at your flying club and again you're allowed to keep taking it until you pass but, since the number of different examination papers is limited, you may become an embarrassment if you fail more than a couple of times. As you have copies of the examination questions to study before the actual examination, the pass mark is quite high: 90%.

The Private Pilot Written Examination

The full written examination is more serious than the other two, partly because it takes place at an official Transport Canada office. Before you can attempt it, you have to get your instructor's recommendation and you must have "attended" 40 hours of Ground School. Although many flying clubs won't tell you, it is actually not essential to attend their Ground School, since there are certified correspondence courses that are an acceptable alternative. However, a large part of the fun of flying is getting to know other pilots at your skill level and a formal, sitting-at-desks Ground School taking 10 or so weeks is an excellent way to meet people.

The official pass mark for this 3 hour examination is 60%, but you may like to set your personal standard higher: I know pilots who have said that, since this examination tests your airmanship and knowledge of air law, they wouldn't be willing to fly unless they scored at least 90%.

The examination is in four parts and individual parts can be repeated after failure if your overall mark is sufficiently high. The four parts are:

≈ Aeronautics and General Knowledge, covering such topics as what makes an aircraft fly, how the basic instruments work and a fascinating topic (if well taught) on human factors, dealing with your attitude to flying as well as the effects of a lack of oxygen at high altitude and other quasi-medical topics.

≈ Air Law. Dull but necessary. This section contains such gems as the minimum altitude at which you may overfly a herd of musk-oxen, as well as more immediately practical knowledge, such as who should give way to whom if you are flying directly towards a tug-plane towing a glider which is itself heading towards a hot-air balloon drifting into the flight path of an airship.

🐝 Meteorology. This is the area which gives most students the most trouble. Predicting the weather is a specialist activity understood by few. It is, however, of crucial importance to pilots as the majority of fatal General Aviation accidents are caused by pilots flying into weather that they cannot handle.

🐝 Navigation. This is fun and probably the easiest part of the examination since you will have previously flown a couple of long cross-country flights.

As with all examinations, particularly multiple-choice ones, knowing the examination techniques is as important as knowing the subject. There are numerous books of exam-type questions available but, unlike the US, there are very few video or computer-based training courses covering the Canadian examination. One computer-based course is produced by Tomvale Air Services Ltd. of Ardoch, Ontario – see their advertisements in the COPA newspaper.

Using Your Licence

Once you have your licence your options are limited only by your wallet and your imagination. This chapter explores a few of the possibilities.

Exploration

My primary interest in recreational flying is exploring Canada and the United States. North America is a large place, and with a Private Pilot Licence you are not even restricted to that continent; a light aircraft journey was recently made to the four extreme points of the American mainland: Cape Froward, Chile, in the south; Joao Pessoa, Brazil, in the east; Boothia Peninsula, Canada, in the north; and Wales, Alaska, in the west. Single-engine flights across the Atlantic are fairly common, particularly to ferry aircraft from one side to the other.

Before you and your passengers start exploring far from your home airport, you will need maps and the two best maps for route planning are the Aeronautical Planning Chart issued by Natural Resources, Canada, and the US Government's IFR/VFR Low Altitude Planning Chart. These charts have the whole of Canada and the whole of the USA on one sheet (albeit on both sides in the case of the US chart) and show all airfields, VORs and distances between the VORs. These charts give you the big picture and help you avoid the always flying east-west syndrome, which comes from looking too often at the standard VFR Navigation Charts (VNCs), which are wide and short. A north-south journey of reasonable length therefore requires a collection of VNC charts, whereas a single chart can accommodate a day's east-west flying.

To fly from Canada into the USA, you need to arrive at an airport with customs and immigration facilities. To find out about these you will need a US equivalent of the *Canada Flight Supplement*; several are available from

Canadian aviation suppliers. I use the *Flight Guide, Airport and Frequency Manual,*[8] but this has the drawback that it is a loose-leaf binder with regular updates which you have to insert manually. This flight-guide also has the disadvantage that airports are ordered by state, meaning that, in order to find an airport, you need first to know which state it is in. The Canada Flight Supplement, in contrast, is a bound book which is discarded and replaced in its entirety and airports are ordered alphabetically, irrespective of their province. While flying in the US, you need to be familiar with small differences in their radio procedures. I have found the small booklet, *VFR Radio Procedures in the USA,*[9] very useful – it contains scripts for flying into every conceivable type of airport and airspace.

Returning to Canada also requires contact with immigration and customs, normally using the so-called CANPASS system, which allows you to land at any CANPASS registered airfield to clear customs, generally without an inspection.

Apart from these administrative details, with your Private Pilot Licence, the world is your oyster. Given the size of the North American continent, an option often worth considering is flying the airlines to a point close to the area you want to explore and then renting an aircraft when you get there. Flying clubs in general will want a check-out flight of an hour or so before letting you loose in one of their aircraft, but this may be better than spending day after day flying, for example, across the prairies to reach the Rockies if you live in Eastern Canada.

Home Building

I have no mechanical ability and no interest in things mechanical. The mechanical world started annoying me when I was given my first bicycle and has continued to irritate me ever since. I therefore see no fun in building an aircraft and my wife is adamant that, should I ever build one, she would never fly in it. I know that I would never fly in it myself, so there's no conflict there.

Having cleared the air with that confession, it must be said that many pilots get a lot of pleasure out of building their own aircraft. The rules are very strict and require that at least 51% of the work in constructing a home-built be carried out by the owner and that the building work be inspected at least twice during construction by a Transport Canada Airworthiness Inspector. The 51% rule is designed to prevent someone from getting a cheap aircraft by buying a kit and then employing a professional company to build it. People often ask why this is disallowed, since a professional company is likely to build a better aircraft than an individual in his or her garage. The answer is that home-built aircraft are registered under the experimental category and the same levels of manufacturing quality are not required for experimental aircraft. Commercial construction of home-builts would mean unfair competition for normal manufacturers.

The Experimental Aircraft Association (see Useful Addresses for EAA for details) gives help to home-builders and has chapters in Alberta, British Columbia, Nova Scotia, Ontario, Prince Edward Island, Quebec and Saskatchewan.

Ultralight Flying

Having no experience in ultralight aircraft, I asked my friend George McKenzie, who flies this type of aircraft, to contribute his enthusiasm. Here is his report:

Most individualists who value an economical way to experience freedom and adventure gravitate to this type of flying. There is nothing quite like the joy of really seeing the countryside slowly glide past as you fly to some quiet destination or an organized fly-in. All of this flying is done outside areas controlled by Air Traffic Control, which means freedom to follow a few simple safety rules while enjoying this wonderful experience, where most fields and lakes are potential landing spots.

Before flying an ultralight, you will need at least an Ultralight Permit. The Ultralight Permit is less expensive to obtain than a Private Pilot Licence or a Recreational Permit, but has limitations, such as not being able to carry any passengers. There are a limited number of convenient ultralight training facilities available, but a list can be found in the <u>Canadian Flight Annual</u>.[10] *Other choices – a Recreational Licence has more benefits and a Private Pilot licence more still. Carrying a passenger in a suitable machine is probably the privilege most pilots appreciate. Both of these licences are available at many flight training schools, using certified aircraft. The benefits of spending an extra couple of thousand dollars are greater flexibility, comfort, safety and confidence. Explore the possibilities, make your choice and enjoy . . . Safely.*

War Birds and Other Classic Aircraft

In the same way that some motorists become fascinated by classic cars, some pilots become fascinated by classic aircraft. There are flying schools that only fly classic aircraft, Tiger Moths for example.

With the raising of the Iron Curtain, a large number of ex-Soviet aircraft are now on the market, being incredibly expensive to run, but great fun.

Aerobatics

I have no experience of aerobatics and therefore asked a colleague, Peter Ashwood-Smith, who enjoys aerobatics, to contribute this paragraph. The enthusiasm is his.

You probably remember the first time you saw the Snowbirds or your first air show. The sight of a jet executing a 4-point roll or a tumbling smoking biplane are the stuff of dreams, but even these pilots had to start somewhere and the experience of controlling a high performance aircraft as it rolls, loops, spins and snaps through the sky is within the grasp of the adventurous private, or even student, pilot, <u>with the appropriate instructor and aircraft</u>. Flying a high performance aerobatic aircraft is one of the most amazing experiences in aviation and if you fly, you owe it to yourself to know what the edge of the envelope (yours and the aircraft's) is really like.

There are other reasons to pursue aerobatics besides the raw fun involved, particularly safety issues. Very few pilots have much experience beyond 60° of bank or pitch and most have little understanding of spins and stalls. Do you have the proper reflexes and reactions to know what to do if your aircraft gets turned upside down? Do you really know what happens after the first revolution of a spin? Do you know the effects of different control inputs during a spin or the effect of giving the inputs in the wrong order? To fly aerobatics solo safely, you have to learn all of the different kinds of spins (upright, inverted, flat, accelerated, etc.) and the proper recovery methods, you have to be able to recognize what type of spin you are in, and quickly and without panic, execute the proper recovery procedure while possibly experiencing several positive or negative Gs, all with the minimum of altitude loss.

Before doing anything more than the spin training normally taken for the Private Pilot Licence, you will need an aircraft rated for aerobatics and an instructor with an Aerobatic Instructor's Rating. These can be hard to find, but a good starting place is with Air Combat Canada. They have a variety of aerobatic programs available in one of the best aerobatic aircraft in the world, the Extra 300L. It's not cheap, but the experience of looping down on your own smoke trail is simply indescribable.

Fly-ins and Social Events

Fly-in breakfasts are an interesting phenomenon. During the summer months airfields nominate a weekend for their fly-in and pilots flock from miles around to eat a substantial breakfast, admire each others' aircraft and chat about flying. That the breakfasts are generally cooked by a chef in a Tilley hat whose claim to fame is his proficiency as a pilot, that the aircraft are the same ones which you saw last weekend at a different fly-in and that the people you're chatting with are the same ones you chatted with a week ago matter not at all; the idea is to have fun and to visit an airfield that you might otherwise not have visited. Of course, when your airfield plays host to a fly-in, you may be the chef, so you can get your own back.

These events are often coupled with competitions of one sort or another: a flour-bombing competition or poker run, for example. A poker run involves flying from airfield to airfield, collecting playing cards at each, to make a poker hand.

The most important "fly-in breakfast" of the year is the week-long event at Oshkosh, Wisconsin, where it is estimated that 20% of all the world's aircraft gather.

Precision Flying and other Competitions

Competitions open to pilots range from flour bombing runs at fly-in breakfasts to the Precision Flying Competitions which a group of pilots, now formed into the Canadian Precision Flying Association, is trying to popularize in Canada.

Flour bombings speak for themselves, but some notes on the Precision Flying Competitions are probably in order. These are very popular in Europe, but are only just catching on over here. They do not involve any form of aerobatics or formation flying, but instead test the basic flying and navigation skills of a pilot in a simple training aircraft.

The competition is typically in three parts:

- using only the manual E6B "computer" and without electronic aids, you are required to calculate headings and ground speeds for your aircraft around a route of 5 or 6 legs, given the anticipated wind speeds and wind direction for the day. This gets the brain cells working and points are lost for inaccuracy.

- without electronic navigation devices, you are required to fly the course, arriving over various checkpoints within 5 seconds of the calculated times. To make this more difficult, you are also expected, simultaneously, to identify the exact location of certain landmarks from photographs provided by the sadistic organizers of the competition.

✄ arriving back at the airport of departure, you then have to demonstrate your skills at precision landings. For this test, a large white line is drawn across the runway and you make three landings – one normal, one without flaps and one without engine or flaps (the engine having supposedly failed). Points are deducted from those pilots who do not get the aircraft's wheels down within an incredibly small distance from the white line.

You may have inferred from this description that I have, once, entered such a competition. It was, I confess, during the precision navigation that I had to descend to read a town name on a water-tower.

Other Ratings and Licences

The Private Pilot Licence is often said to be a licence to start learning. Many pilots see it as an end in itself, while others see it as a springboard to other ratings: particularly the night rating and the float-plane rating. As emphasized in a previous chapter, the Instrument Rating provides useful, additional training even for the recreational pilot.

Other Sources of Information

There are numerous magazines, mainly published in the USA, which address the possibilities of what to do once you have your licence. Choice of magazine depends on personal prejudices and interests. I dislike one magazine from the USA because it recounts interesting flights made to various parts of that country, *but never includes a map*. Unless you have an intimate knowledge of USA geography, which I haven't, it's difficult to know where the flights are taking place. Another magazine, oriented towards flight training, perpetually abbreviates MegaHertz in radio frequencies as mHz (i.e., milliHertz) rather than MHz. This may not irritate you, but an error of 1 000 000 000 times irritates me and makes me wonder about the accuracy of the other terms they use.

I regularly buy the US magazine *Flying* and the UK magazine *Pilot*, both available in most larger Canadian magazine shops, since these publications seem to balance articles about interesting journeys flown (with maps in the case of *Pilot*), reviews of aircraft and new gadgets, and reminiscences from experienced pilots. One criticism that I have of all flying magazines is the amount of space devoted to analyzing accidents. The COPA newsletter even has a column insensitively called "Crash Corner." I understand that the most dangerous vehicle is the horse, yet magazines about horse-back riding are not full of articles about broken legs; aviation magazines seem obsessed with accidents and injuries. The excuse is that accident reports are published to allow pilots to learn from others' mistakes. To some extent this is valid; the incident reprinted on page 43, for example, is a salutary reminder to check the fuel tanks before take-off, but many examples seem more voyeuristic than educational.

In addition to these magazines, I continually read and re-read a number of good books about flying; some are classics like Ernest K. Gann's *Fate is the Hunter*,[11] some are biographies of Canadian bush pilots like Ronald Keith's *Bush Pilot with a Briefcase*[12] and Lewis Leigh's *And I Shall Fly*[13] and some are teach-yourself books like Donald Clausing's *Improve Your Flying Skills*[14] and Richard Collins' *Flying the Weather Map*.[15]

Collins' book is particularly useful, as it covers a topic which most pilots find very difficult, the weather. For the Private Pilot Licence you will have to study the weather and answer examination questions on it, but the topic is so enormous that a prudent pilot continues learning. At first, after you get your licence, you may only fly on really perfect days but, as time passes, you will inevitably meet adverse weather and Collins' book contains analyses of 46 flights he actually flew, with details of the weather map before he left and the actual conditions he met *en route*. A very clear but more theoretical analysis of the weather is given in Tom Bradbury's book *Meteorology and Flight: A Pilot's Guide to Weather*.[16] This book is aimed primarily at glider pilots, who have an even closer interest in the weather than power pilots, but contains a very lucid general explanation of weather systems. Environment Canada also publishes a book on weather for pilots,[17] which I find very poor and over-priced.

In addition to printed books, there are numerous World-Wide Web sites related to aviation. Three useful starting points are: the site associated with *Pilot Magazine* (http://www.hiway.co.uk/pilot); http://www.landings.com; and http://www.avweb.com.

A Sample Flight

The shops are full of books describing heroic and dangerous flights by war-time aces and Canadian bush pilots. This is not one of them. This chapter describes an actual flight that I undertook with friends, where no heroics were required and no desperate situations were overcome by magnificent flying skills. Insofar as any flight is "normal," this was a normal flight as flown a thousand times a week by recreational pilots in Canada and I include it here to illustrate what actually happens during a flight. The characters in this story are my wife Alison, fellow pilot Laurie Davis, his wife Elva, his aircraft CHARLIE GOLF X-RAY BRAVO UNIFORM (C-GXBU) and myself.

Meeting on the Friday evening before a long weekend, we decided to take Laurie's aircraft, a Piper Cherokee, from Rockcliffe, an uncontrolled airport in the north of Ottawa, to Quebec City the following day. Laurie was to fly there, with me navigating, we would stay overnight and then I was to fly back with Laurie as navigator. XBU is not certified for IFR flying and so we were to fly VFR.

On Saturday morning we phoned the local Flight Service Station to be told that the cold front which had passed Ottawa eastwards during the night had not cleared through as quickly as expected. Ottawa was clear but east of Montreal the weather was not suitable for VFR flight.

The flexibility of recreational flying was apparent when Elva suggested changing our destination to Stratford, Ontario, west of Toronto, a town none of us had previously visited. We agreed and consulted the Canada Flight Supplement (CFS), which gave us the necessary information, including the runways (05 and 23 in this case), the radio frequency (122.8 MHz), the distance of the town from the airport (2 miles) and a note of caution that deer occasionally cross the runway. This book is a mine of interesting information. Once, when staying overnight in Grand Falls, New Brunswick, either Alison or I left all our reading matter in the aircraft, some kilometers from the motel (there is still some dispute as to which of us was responsible for this). That evening, desperate for something to read, I found a copy of the Canada Flight Supplement in my flight bag and read it cover-to-cover. It contains information, for example, on how to intercept a Russian fighter and on all types of jet aircraft starting units.

So we prepared to fly to Stratford and I, as navigator, filed our flight plan with the Flight Service Station while Laurie carried out the pre-flight inspection: checking the aircraft and getting it ready. Laurie has programmed his computer to calculate flight information given the route and wind conditions, which speeds up the planning process enormously. Similar programs are freely available from the Internet and many companies produce commercial packages, but writing one's own is fun. Laurie's program also calculates the aircraft's weight-and-balance report given the weights of the pilot, passengers and luggage. An aircraft's manufacturer specifies the maximum weight that it can lift and how that weight may be distributed. If the aircraft is overloaded, then it will perform poorly, perhaps not even becoming airborne from the runway. If the weight is too far back, then the aircraft can become unstable and difficult, if not impossible, to fly.

I prefer to fly from VOR to VOR rather than use the GPS and, as navigator, I filed a route which we could fly using our VOR receivers. One error I made was not to check Notices to Airpersons (NOTAMs) for our route as well as for our destination. NOTAMs are temporary notices issued to say that an airport or runway is closed, taxiway lines are being repainted or, most importantly for this flight, navigation devices are out-of-service.

Having two pilots in an aircraft that only needs one can be dangerous (imagine driving at speed in a car with two steering wheels), but Laurie and I divide the work up: one person only is pilot-in-command and flies the aircraft and the other navigates and works the radio. The potential problem with two pilots, of course, is that each will defer to the other if a dangerous situation arises, because neither wants to be thought critical of the other pilot's ability. Two instructors flying together are even more dangerous. Luckily, Laurie and I have no reservations about criticizing each other's flying abilities and we have talked through on many occasions the roles each of us would play in the event of an engine failure. I once had the honor of flying from Peterborough, Ontario, to Ottawa with four pilots in the aircraft, two with instrument ratings. In spite of having three GPSs and a full suite of instrument navigation equipment, we actually got lost (momentarily) while describing to each other the advantages of our own particular method of navigation.

We took off on our flight to Stratford, and, as radio operator, I spoke to the Gatineau Flight Service Station to open our flight plan. This meant that Search and Rescue would automatically start if we didn't arrive in Stratford. The Flight Service Stations throughout Canada also offer various services to aircraft in flight, including weather updates.

This is perhaps the moment to mention one embarrassment lurking behind the radio: the *stuck microphone*. The aviation radio system is very primitive and only one pilot may speak at a time on any frequency. If two pilots start to transmit at the same time, then nothing but a nasty, squawking noise emerges. When a pilot pushes the TALK button, speaks and then releases it, it sometimes sticks on. This not only prevents anyone else from transmitting on that frequency, it also ensures that all cockpit conversation is broadcast to everyone listening. I once gave all aircraft within 50 miles of Ottawa a personal aerial tour of the Gatineau Park by not noticing that my microphone button had stuck down. Radio manufacturers are now coming to grips with this problem and modern radios have a cut-out, which electronically cuts the microphone button off after 35 seconds or so.

After opening the flight plan, I contacted Ottawa Air Traffic Control (ATC) and they issued us with a SQUAWK code, a unique 4-digit number, which we dialed into our transponder.

> OTTAWA TERMINAL, THIS IS PIPER CHEROKEE GOLF X-RAY BRAVO UNIFORM OUT OF ROCKCLIFFE PASSING 2000 FEET

> X-RAY BRAVO UNIFORM, SQUAWK 1234 . . . X-RAY BRAVO UNIFORM RADAR IDENTIFIED 5 WEST OF ROCKCLIFFE AT 2500 FEET, STATE INTENTIONS

> X-RAY BRAVO UNIFORM VFR TO STRATFORD AT 4500 FEET

> X-RAY BRAVO UNIFORM CLIMB AT YOUR DISCRETION, MAINTAIN VFR AT ALL TIMES

The aircraft's transponder responds to interrogations by ATC's radar with the number dialed in and this labels our dot on the radar screen with XBU's identity and altitude. Work load permitting, ATC would now advise us of other aircraft flying near us. When flying VFR, it is up to the pilot, and not ATC, to look out for other aircraft. Having said this, the folks in Ottawa do seem to be able to warn VFR pilots of other aircraft most of the time. I know from personal experience that the radar that ATC uses is sufficiently sensitive to notice an aircraft flying in a circle, such as the one I flew when returning to Rockcliffe one day in order to show a passenger something on the ground. I was embarrassed by a query from ATC asking whether we were OK. If ATC does notice an aircraft near you, they will point it out in a message such as:

> X-RAY BRAVO UNIFORM, CESSNA TRAFFIC AT 3 O'CLOCK, 3000 FEET NORTH-EAST BOUND

and you look for the other aircraft and reply

OTTAWA TERMINAL, X-RAY BRAVO UNIFORM HAS THE TRAFFIC [in sight]

These exchanges characterize the grammar-less use of formalized English used to reduce time on the radio and ensure that the message gets through when the channel is poor.

By the time we had our squawk code dialed in, Laurie had flown to the VOR just north-west of Ottawa and was flying south-west along a radial directly away from it. After about 15 minutes, Ottawa ATC contacted us to say that we were leaving their radar coverage and, effectively, that we were on our own. We then invoked another service which is always available to IFR traffic, but only to VFR traffic if ATC's workload permits: we asked for *Flight Following*. This requested that, although we had fallen off Ottawa's local radar screen, Toronto ATC continue to follow us on their wider-area radar. There was a short delay while Ottawa telephoned Toronto and requested this on our behalf. Ottawa then came back to us with a radio frequency that we could use to contact Toronto. I have never actually had a request for Flight Following turned down and I imagine that the controllers would rather have a labeled dot moving across their screens, one they can contact if necessary, than an unlabeled dot.

With Toronto Centre watching our every move on radar, we continued away from the Ottawa VOR to the next VOR in the chain, that at Coehill, just north of Trenton. I was also watching ground features and following our progress on the map and this was as well because, when we tried to receive the Coehill VOR we couldn't get a signal. Gradually we lost the signals from the Ottawa VOR and were still unable to pick up Coehill. Yes, I should have asked for the NOTAMs for the *en route* navigational devices: Coehill was switched off for maintenance. It didn't matter, and by ded reckoning we actually flew over it and saw it on the ground, but it was a reminder for another day. Every flight has such lessons to be learned.

Our course took us just north of Toronto and ATC asked us to descend to 2000 feet for a few miles as we passed across the flight-path into Pearson airport. As we left the Toronto area, a gliding field was marked on the chart and a wave of nostalgia overtook me as, off our right wing, I saw several gliders thermalling.

About 10 miles from Stratford we contacted the airport operator (known as UNICOM) to get advice about which runway to use.

STRATFORD UNICOM, THIS IS PIPER CHEROKEE GOLF X-RAY BRAVO UNIFORM

X-RAY BRAVO UNIFORM, GO AHEAD

STRATFORD, X-RAY BRAVO UNIFORM IS 10 [miles] EAST AT 4500 [feet] INBOUND FOR LANDING, REQUESTING AIRPORT ADVISORIES

ROGER, X-RAY BRAVO UNIFORM, WINDS ARE FROM THE EAST AT 5 KNOTS, RUNWAY 05 IS PREFERRED, NO REPORTED TRAFFIC IN CIRCUIT

There is genuine significance in some of these words in Stratford's replies: Stratford being an uncontrolled airport, it is the pilot's decision which runway to use and the UNICOM operator can only offer *advice*. Nor can the operator say that there is no other traffic in the circuit, since there may be aircraft there without radios; he can, however, say that there is no *reported* traffic. Getting an answer from the UNICOM operator is unusual at many uncontrolled airports (and even some airports in the USA which claim to be "International"). Quite often the whole airport is deserted and an incoming pilot has to fly over the field to look down at the wind-sock before deciding which runway to use.

Whether the UNICOM operator gives airport advisories or not, the incoming pilot, for safety's sake, is expected to report his presence to any other aircraft that might be in the vicinity, either on the ground or in the air:

STRATFORD TRAFFIC, PIPER CHEROKEE X-RAY BRAVO UNIFORM IS EIGHT [miles] EAST DESCEND-ING THROUGH 2000 FEET FOR CIRCUIT HEIGHT. WILL JOIN STRAIGHT-IN LEFT-HAND DOWN-WIND FOR RUNWAY 05 . . .

STRATFORD TRAFFIC, X-RAY BRAVO UNIFORM IS ESTABLISHED LEFT-HAND DOWN-WIND FOR RUN-WAY 05 . . .

STRATFORD TRAFFIC, X-RAY BRAVO UNIFORM IS FINAL FOR RUNWAY 05, FULL STOP

The "FULL STOP" in the last radio call indicates that XBU is going to land and come to a complete stop, rather than immediately take-off again (i.e., do a "touch-and-go").

One question that worried me when I was learning was "how do I get out of an airport, particularly a large international one, after I've landed?" When arriving on a commercial flight, one is shepherded through tunnels, customs, etc. and emerges in the parking lot. How is this achieved if you're flying in by yourself? Where do you park the aircraft? The answer is that, at the larger airports, there are normally several Fixed Base Operators (FBOs) run by the fuel companies. They will refuel the aircraft, tie it down for the night and generally make you very welcome. Montreal Mirabel goes one step further, providing a Gate and 150-person bus to carry the pilot and passengers to and from the terminal building, all without fee.

We stayed overnight in Stratford, a delightful town, although we arrived on a day when there was nothing playing in the theatre, and awoke the next morning to find a mist over the entire area, making an early departure impossible. Visibility was certainly sufficient for an IFR takeoff and the journey under IFR would have been easy, but less fun, than flying VFR. If you have a need to get from A to B on a particular day at a particular time, then you need your Instrument Rating.

We walked around the town until mid-morning and then made a leisurely journey out to the airport. We decided that, rather than flying directly back to Ottawa, we would deviate to the north to land for lunch at Orillia, on the eastern shore of Lake Simcoe.

Laurie, as navigator this time, filed a flight plan with a stop in Orillia while I did the pre-flight checks. These include checking the level of the fuel in the tanks visually, checking that no water has crept into the fuel, checking the oil level in the engine and numerous other small items.

Flying seems to revolve around check-lists: there are pre-flight inspection checklists, engine-start checklists, engine run-up checklists, pre-landing checklists, post-landing checklists and engine shut-off checklists. You are taught not to learn these checklists, since that is how items are forgotten, and recently I was reminded how strange this seems to non-pilots. Ottawa and Rockcliffe Flying Clubs hold a flying day each year when local pilots give rides, primarily to children, for charity. I had three youngsters in my aircraft and was going through the engine-runup checklist, mumbling the items to myself as I did it, when the bright young thing in the passenger seat beside me asked, "Are you a beginner at flying?" I was puzzled by the question and answered that I wasn't. It was only later that I realized what had provoked the question: she had seen and heard me work my way aloud through three check-lists and had interpreted them as "how to fly" instructions.

By the time we were ready in Stratford, the mist had more-or-less been burned off by the sun and we took off and climbed to 3000 feet Above Sea Level (ASL).

As we flew along, clouds started to build beneath us. Initially these were well broken and we flew above them, still seeing the ground clearly. As we approached Borden, near Lake Simcoe, the gaps between the clouds became smaller and, as we were flying according to Visual Flight Rules, we had to descend to keep the ground in sight. We continued on towards Lake Simcoe and found ourselves descending further and further to stay below the clouds. Navigation charts mark safe heights, heights above which no natural or man-made obstacles are known. We eventually descended to that height and visibility had reduced to a few miles.

Deciding that it would be impossible to get into Orillia, we chose to fly to the nearest reasonably large airport and wait for things to improve. Here even I, VOR-to-VOR navigator that I am, must admit that the GPS was extremely useful. Laurie punched the GO TO NEAREST button and we immediately had a moving map, countdown of distance and estimated time to Muskoka airport. Laurie radioed ahead to Muskoka to find the weather there and was told that the sky was clear! At that time we were 10 miles away flying at 1600 feet under a solid overcast. We radioed our intention to land at Muskoka and almost immediately flew out from under the clouds into a

The Clouds Behind Us. Photo by Alison Hobbs

clear sky. I immediately climbed, Alison took a photograph of the cloud layer, now behind us, and Laurie again contacted Muskoka to tell them of our change of plan: no landing at Muskoka after all.

Having abandoned the stop-over in Orillia, we were now flying along a route different from that on our flight plan, so Laurie contacted the Toronto Flight Service Station to change our route and estimated time of arrival at Rockcliffe.

The rest of the journey was uneventful: as we approached Ottawa we again contacted ATC and were again issued with a squawk code for our transponder. As we approached Rockcliffe, Ottawa ATC told us to transfer to the Rockcliffe UNICOM frequency. After landing we remembered, once again, to close our flight plan. This return trip illustrated the advantage of an Instrument Rating. I am certified to fly in Instrument Meteorological Conditions (IMC), but Laurie's aircraft isn't. Had it been, then my reaction to the increasing cloud cover would have been to file an IFR Flight Plan from the air and continue above rather than below the cloud layer. We were never in danger, but pilots have been known to get into trouble by continuing to descend below the safe altitude as the clouds drop; it is much simpler, safer and faster to file IFR, if you are legally able, and fly through and above them.

Glossary

Glossaries are often of the type which tell you, correctly, that VFR stands for Visual Flight Rules and then leave you little the wiser. I hope that this glossary, used together with the index which follows, will do more, by explaining the terms. Note that some of the terms included in this glossary have not been used in the text: they are included here because they are commonly-used terms that the new pilot will hear around the flying club.

Adages. Flying is full of wise sayings repeated to newcomers by old-timers. Don't be fooled into thinking them original. Some examples are:

- There's nothing as useless as runway behind you (*so taxi to the very beginning of the runway before taking off*).

- There's nothing as useless as height above you (*so don't fly low and certainly don't fly slow and low*).

- There's nothing as useless as fuel in the bowser (fuel tanker).

- The only time you can have too much fuel is when you are on fire (*always fill up when you have the opportunity; it may take you longer to get to your destination than you think*).

- Aviate, Navigate, Communicate (*when you're in trouble in the air, first concentrate on flying the aircraft, then decide where you're going and only then use the radio to declare an emergency, inform others of your predicament, etc.*).

- High to low, watch out below (*when you fly from an area of higher air pressure into an area of lower pressure then your altimeter will read too high: you are flying closer to the ground than you think*).

- Time spent flying is not deducted from your life span.

⚔ There are old pilots and bold pilots, but no old, bold pilots.

⚔ A good pilot uses superior judgement to avoid getting into situations which require superior skill.

⚔ It's better to be down wishing you were up rather than up wishing you were down.

ADF. Automatic Direction Finder. An instrument in the aircraft which points a needle towards a Non-Direction Beacon (NDB) on the ground.

AGL. Above Ground Level, a good place to be when flying.

AIP. Aeronautical Information Publication. A document published by Transport Canada Aviation containing useful extracts from air law together with advice on airmanship.[18]

Airspeed. An aircraft flies through the air and the instruments in the cockpit, other than the GPS, display the speed that the aircraft is moving through the air. This is normally not the speed at which the aircraft is moving across the ground. If, for example, an aircraft is flying with an airspeed of 100 knots into a head wind of 10 knots, then its ground speed will be 90 knots. The GPS, being unaware of local winds, measures ground speed.

Altimeter. A device in the cockpit of an aircraft which ostensibly measures your height above sea level. Actually it measures air pressure and this can cause problems. As you know from weather maps, atmospheric pressure varies from place to place as LOW and HIGH pressure areas move around. You should set the altimeter to the local barometric pressure on the ground before you depart and, as you fly along, reset the altimeter regularly to the local barometric pressure. It is particularly dangerous when you fly from a high pressure area into a low pressure area without resetting the altimeter. Take, for example, the case where a HIGH pressure of 30.15 inches of mercury (yes – pilots use inches of mercury to record atmospheric pressure rather than millibars!) is positioned over your departure airfield and you correctly set this on the altimeter before departure. You fly for a few hours and arrive at an airport where the pressure is 28.65 inches of mercury. If you have not reset the altimeter, it will now be reading 750 feet too high and you will be flying 750 feet lower than you think. If the weather is clear and you can see the local hills, this may not be too much of a problem, but if the weather is marginal and you have descended to stay below cloud, this could mean the difference between a pleasant flight and Controlled Flight into Terrain (CFIT). Flight Service Stations along your route provide you with up-to-date pressure readings.

AME. Aircraft Maintenance Engineer. A person legally able to carry out maintenance on an aircraft and sign off that maintenance as having been done. Finding a good AME is like striking gold.

ASL. Above sea level.

ATC. Air Traffic Control. A group of highly-trained people, mostly working underground, following your flight on radar screens. They will clear you into controlled airspace, advise you of other aircraft flying near you and generally watch over your flight if you talk to them nicely.

ATIS. Automatic Terminal Information Service. This is a message, recorded each hour onto tape at the larger airports and broadcast repeatedly to tell incoming aircraft about the weather and special conditions (runways in use, etc.) at the airport.

Banking. In order to turn, an aircraft tips to one side slightly to direct part of its lift into the centre of a circle. This is known as banking and I am no longer surprised when I see a totally erroneous explanation of this in aviation text books. The ideas are not difficult and, for the sake of completeness, are recorded here. When you do your ground school, you will probably get a totally different picture. That picture is wrong. The most popular ground school text book, *From the Ground Up*,[19] has an excellent diagram, but then blows it by giving an erroneous description.

The simple fact, known to all physicists but few pilots, is that when an object is going around in a circle, the forces acting on it are not balanced and there is a net force *towards the centre of the circle.* If you imagine being swung around in a circle by someone holding your arm, you can imagine the force towards the centre of the circle pulling your arm out of joint. There is *no* force acting outwards on you at all.

Now consider the aircraft in the left-most diagram in the figure on the next page. It is flying in a straight line at constant altitude, the wings are giving lift and this lift is equal to the weight of the aircraft. The aircraft therefore moves neither up nor down.

In the centre diagram, the aircraft now banks. Neither the weight nor the lift from the wings changes at all and the weight still acts downwards and the lift still acts perpendicularly to the wings. So far, so good.

Now, instead of a single lift from the wings, we can draw this force as two forces as shown on the right of figure. There are no new forces here: the single lift force has simply been split into two. This right-hand figure shows two things:

✄ the force acting upwards is smaller than it was when the aircraft was in straight flight so, unless you pull back a little bit on the control column, the aircraft will start to descend.

there is an unbalanced force towards the right. The aircraft will therefore turn in a circle towards the right. This is called the *centripetal* force.

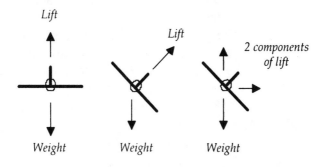

Forces During Banking

I apologize for getting emotional about this, but I see it mis-taught time after time and it really isn't that difficult.

While on the subject of aviation tales, perhaps I should mention the notorious *down-wind turn*. This canard raises its head in the aviation magazines regularly and goes as follows: imagine that you are flying north at 100 knots into a head-wind of 40 knots. You will be flying over the ground at 60 knots. Apart from relativistic effects, so far so good. Now assume that you turn with a perfectly banked turn through 180 degrees to head south. The aircraft now has a tail-wind of 40 knots and is passing across the ground at 140 knots. The aircraft apparently has to speed up from 60 to 140 knots and while doing so, all sorts of terrible things may happen to it. Precisely what these terrible things are differs from account to account, but they normally involve stalling.

The best rebuttal of this strange (and completely erroneous) argument was probably that in the Air Mail section of *Pilot* magazine for May 1996 (see their web page. In simple terms, even if there were no wind, an aircraft making a 180° turn at 100 knots will experience a change in ground speed of 200 knots (100 knots north to 100 knots south) and this is exactly the same as a turn in the 40 knot wind (from 60 knots north to 140 knots south – a difference of 200 knots in each case). I once offered publicly to eat my aircraft, GPS and all, if any advocate of the erroneous idea would take the simple test of detecting the difference between an upwind and a downwind turn when blindfolded. No one took me up on the challenge.

Call Sign. Each aircraft has a unique call sign. In Canada this consists of the letter C followed by an F or G and then three more letters. One of the aircraft I fly is C-FPTN which, over the radio, is called FOXTROT, PAPA, TANGO, NOVEMBER in the phonetic alphabet. Normally, if GOLF, PAPA, TANGO, NOVEMBER is not flying at the same time, then the controller will abbreviate the call sign to PAPA, TANGO, NOVEMBER or even TANGO NOVEMBER.

CANPASS. A system whereby a pilot in a small aircraft returning to Canada from the USA can clear customs and immigration at an airport without a customs and immigration office. The pilot is required to telephone Canadian customs before departing for Canada and give a time and place of arrival. The customs inspector will then either drive out to the airport of arrival or, more commonly, will issue a clearance number on arrival without an inspection. There is a similar policy, known as GATE, for Canadian citizens flying into the USA.

CAP. Canada Air Pilot. See the glossary entry for "plates."

CAVOK. This term is pronounced cav-oh-kay rather than cav-ock. It has a precise meteorological meaning, but is normally used by pilots to mean that the ceiling (cloud base) is high and the visibility is good. The term means, "no need to worry about the clouds and visibility."

Ceiling. This term has two different meanings. In a weather report or forecast, the ceiling is the height at which there is broken or overcast cloud. Thus a ceiling of 2000 feet officially means that more than 63% of the sky is covered with cloud at 2000 feet above the ground. For an aircraft, its ceiling is effectively the highest that it can fly.

Checkpoint. A position at which a pilot, when flying cross-country, records the time, calculates the aircraft's ground speed, estimates the time to the next way point and the time to the end of the flight. Checkpoints are chosen before the flight as places easily distinguishable from the air: perhaps a distinctive lake or river.

CFI. In the USA this means "certified flying instructor" (i.e., a normal flying instructor), whereas in Canada and elsewhere it means "Chief Flying Instructor." Reading references to CFIs in magazines from the USA puzzled me for a long time until I realized this simple difference. There will be one Chief Flying Instructor at each flying school and he or she will be responsible for overall flight training safety and standards.

CFIT. Controlled Flight into Terrain. The act of flying a completely functional aircraft into the ground, probably due to loss of orientation.

Circuit. When an aircraft approaches an uncontrolled airport (i.e., one without a control tower), it flies a circuit, i.e., the pattern that all aircraft will be flying. This has two advantages: firstly, since everyone is flying the same circuit, it is easier to predict where other aircraft will be, and secondly, landing at a strange airfield is easier if you have a set point in the circuit at which to do things.

I found this out flying into Toronto City Centre airport soon after getting my licence. This is a controlled airport and, rather than flying a circuit, I was cleared to land "straight-in." I was used to flying over top of the airport, descending to 1000 feet above ground, turning downwind (see figure below) and doing my landing checks, turning base and putting my flaps down, etc. Being cleared straight-in meant that I could land directly on the runway ahead of me. I had a terrible job to assess whether I was too high or not (even with the VASIS lights to help) and just before touchdown I realized that I was landing with my flaps up. This was not serious, but it indicated how closely I'd associated putting the flaps down to a particular point in the circuit: it was somewhat alarming at the time.

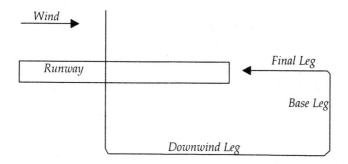

A Left-Hand Circuit

COPA. Canadian Owners' and Pilots' Association. A group which lobbies governments and other organizations on behalf of pilots and General Aviation.

Dead Reckoning. See glossary entry for *ded reckoning*.

Ded Reckoning. Short for Deduced Reckoning: the technique of navigating by calculating bearings and using a stop watch. This technique can be remarkably accurate, bringing in checkpoints 15 or 20 minutes apart within a few seconds of the predicted times. With the advent of the Global Positioning System, this skill is falling into disuse among some pilots, but it will always be a useful backup when other techniques fail.

DME. Distance Measuring Equipment. Strictly, a device fitted in an aircraft which can calculate the distance to special radio transmitters, normally installed alongside VORs. The term is also used to indicate distance from an airport or navigation device, even when GPS or map reading is being used rather than an actual DME: "PAPA TANGO NOVEMBER is currently 34 DME from Ottawa."

E6B. A circular slide rule used by pilots before flight to estimate the direction in which they should point the aircraft and during flight to calculate their ground speed and time to destination. Like most modern pilots, when I first met the E6B, I mocked it. Electronic calculators exist which do everything the E6B does and more. In an examination the electronic versions are excellent, as they give more accurate answers more quickly. In flight I reverted to the manual E6B soon after passing my flight test, it being easier to use (really) and actually quicker in operation.

EAA. Experimental Aircraft Association. The Association which offers help, advice and encouragement to pilots building their own aircraft, in addition to providing a number of programs and scholarships to support aviation generally.

ELT. Emergency Locator Transmitter. A device normally fitted behind the rear seats in an aircraft, which automatically transmits on the international distress frequency (121.5 MHz) if the aircraft crashes. The signals are picked up by passing satellites or overflying aircraft and alert the emergency services. Today's ELTs were not really designed for satellite detection and only give a very poor definition of the downed aircraft's location. New standards and new ELTs are to be introduced early in the 21st century.

Briefing inexperienced passengers, possibly making their first flight in anything smaller than a Boeing 747, on the ELT is one of the most diplomatic things a pilot has to do (the other being asking passengers for their weight so that you can calculate the aircraft's Weight-and-Balance). What you need to say is something like "... and in the baggage compartment there's a device called an ELT. If we crash and I'm killed and you aren't, then, although it should have come on automatically, it's in your best interests to crawl over there and switch it to ON." This can have a first-time passenger reaching for the door handle and getting out before you're finished. I normally compromise with the weasel words " . . . and in the baggage compartment there's a device called an ELT. If we're forced down off-airport and I'm incapacitated, you should switch it to ON."

Experimental Aircraft. The official term for a home-built aircraft.

FBO. Fixed Base Operator. A strange description of a very useful service. At all the major airports, the fuel companies establish bases to tempt you to buy fuel from them. These bases have a pilots' lounge with flight planning tools, weather services and telephones. They also have free coffee, muffins and lounges in which your passengers can relax in reclining chairs with their feet up while you plan the flight. The FBO often provides a courtesy bus to the nearest town and, on one occasion when the courtesy bus was not available, I was given the FBO manager's car keys to drive myself into town for a meal. I always feel guilty at having all this service in return for buying $50 of fuel, but I assume they think I might be back next week with my Executive Jet.

FIR. Flight Information Region. For providing flight information services, Canada is divided into seven Flight Information Regions: Gander Oceanic, Gander Domestic, Moncton, Montreal, Toronto, Winnipeg, Edmonton and Vancouver. See page 15 for the special linguistic attributes within the Montreal FIR.

Flaps. The shape of any aircraft wing is a compromise: for fast flight it needs to be thin and for slow flight (taking off and landing) it needs to be greatly curved. Flaps are devices which can be lowered on the back of the wing to increase its curvature, particularly during landing. Flaps are normally controlled by electrical motors, but I fly two aircraft with hand-operated flap levers rather like a hand-brake lever in a car. At first I found manual operation cumbersome and distracting at a time when I least needed distractions, lining up to land, but now I have a certain affection for this primitive system, since at least it has no motor to burn out.

Piper Cherokee C-GXBU landing with full flaps.

Flight Following. A service provided by Air Traffic Control, if their workload permits, whereby they will follow an aircraft on their radar screen and, again if workload permits, point out any other aircraft flying nearby.

Flight Plan. Strictly speaking, if you fly more than 25 nautical miles from your base, you are required to file a Flight Plan with a Flight Service Station or leave a Flight Itinerary with a responsible person. These have details of your aircraft, where you are flying and when you expect to arrive. When you arrive, you make another call to a Flight Service Station to close the plan. Forgetting to close a Flight Plan is a pilot's recurring nightmare. Once your arrival time has passed, without Flight Services having heard from you, they start a radio search, contacting your destination airport, airports that you are likely to have flown over and spoken to, etc. If they can't find you, then Search and Rescue is notified and a real (and costly) search begins. On a long flight a pilot will radio position reports to a nearby Flight Service Station at intervals so that, should a search be necessary, those searching will know where to begin.

Many pilots don't file Flight Plans and this is daft, as the service is free and, provided you remember to close the plan once you're on the ground, almost effortless. It gives you peace of mind to know that someone will be looking for you if you are unlucky. The only real drawback is on those really nice flying days when I take off without a really clear idea of where I'm going.

Foggles. These are devices similar to spectacles, which you wear to prevent you from being able to see anything except the aircraft's instruments.

FSS. Flight Service Station. Before flying you will need to check on the weather, file a flight plan and check whether your destination airport is open. In flight you will need regular weather updates and will want to file position reports to help potential search teams. A

Flight Service Station specialist will help you with all of these. The specialists are trained to interpret the weather and accept your flight plan. A Flight Service Station can always be reached in Canada by dialling 1-800-INFO-FSS.

G forces. These are more accurately "g-accelerations." The symbol g is the acceleration with which a body falls to the earth if dropped (for example, cannon balls off the leaning tower of Pisa). The force pulling a body towards the earth (its *weight*) depends on g. On the moon, g is smaller and you weigh less. When performing aerobatics the pilot may perform a manoeuvre which causes the aircraft to accelerate upwards. This adds to g and makes you feel heavier. When going over the top of a loop, the aircraft is accelerating downwards (towards the centre of the circle) and this acceleration subtracts from g, making you feel lighter (and possibly sick). Pilots talk of "negative-g" to mean accelerations downwards causing the pilot and passengers to feel lighter than normal, and "positive-g" to mean accelerations upwards causing the pilot to feel heavier.

GATE. See glossary entry for *CANPASS*.

General Aviation. A term used to mean private and recreational flying as distinct from flying with the commercial airlines.

Go-around. See the glossary entry for overshoot.

GPS. Global Positioning System. This is a set of satellites launched by the US Military which are continually transmitting very accurate time signals. A GPS receiver, which costs anywhere from $400 to $2000 depending on its features, receives these signals and deduces its position from the delays. Most units display moving maps showing the receiver's position relative to protected airspace, runways, etc. Currently, the signals from the satellites have deliberate errors introduced by the US Military to avoid giving very accurate positions to enemy missiles, reducing their accuracy to about 30m. The US Military, which owns these satellites, has agreed to remove this deliberate error before 2008. The equivalent Russian system, GLONASS, does not have this error.

There is some concern about the ease of knocking out the GPS coverage in an area, and all but the most trusting pilots are continuing to keep their antique VOR and ADF receivers even after they have installed GPS.

Greaser. The landing every pilot dreams of. The aircraft touches down so smoothly that the passengers are not even aware that the aircraft has stopped flying.

Ground speed. The speed at which an aircraft is travelling across the ground, normally measured in knots (qv). See the glossary entry for Airspeed.

Headset. The engine noise within a light aircraft is quite high and most pilots wear headsets during flight. These allow conversation between the pilot and passengers using the intercom and radio conversation between the pilot and ATC.

Hood. A device used during training to cover your eyes so that you can see the instruments but not out of the window.

IFR. Instrument Flight Rules. The rules which you must follow if you are flying without being able to see the ground. In order to be able to fly in accordance with IFR, special training, a flight test and examination are required. See the glossary entry for VFR.

ILS. Instrument Landing System. A device installed at the larger airports which allows you to line an aircraft up with the runway centre line (using the localizer part of the ILS) and to descend in such a manner that the aircraft will land on the runway (using the glide-slope part of the ILS) even if you are in cloud. Inside the aircraft, you tune to the correct frequency and then try to keep two cross-hairs in the centre of a circle. When the horizontal cross-hair moves up or down from the centre it indicates that you are too low or too high. When the vertical cross-hair moves left or right of the middle you are too far to the right or left. In theory, keeping the needles correctly centred would allow you to take the aircraft right down to the runway but, in practice, unless the airport and aircraft have special equipment and you have special training, the last 200 feet to the runway have to be flown visually – if you cannot see the runway or runway lights when 200 feet from the ground, you are required to abort the landing.

IMC. Instrument Meteorological Conditions. Weather conditions where the visibility is too bad for a pilot to be able to fly in accordance with the Visual Flight Rules, i.e., while seeing the ground and staying clear of cloud.

Knot. A pre-historic nautical term meaning "one nautical mile per hour" (about 2 km/hr). Flying has taken a lot of terms from ships (cockpit, pilot, captain, navigator, MAYDAY, rudder, red and green lights, etc.) and "knot" is one of the more unlikely. Training aircraft typically fly at speeds of 80 to 120 knots (148 to 222 km/hr). The nautical mile does have some small justification, as it is the distance between two minutes of latitude and so can be read easily from a navigation chart.

METAR. A routine weather report issued hourly from an airport to say what the weather is *at the time of issue*. It is not a forecast and does not, therefore, predict what the weather is going to be at any time in the future. See the glossary entry for TAF.

NDB. Non-Directional Beacon. A radio transmitter that a receiver in an aircraft (called an ADF) can detect and towards which it can point a needle.

NOTAM. In these politically correct days, this acronym stands for "Notices to Airpersons" and should therefore be NOTAP, but the aviation world seems to take political correctness so far and no further. A NOTAM is issued when something unusual has happened: an airport is unexpectedly closed for a period, an airshow is taking place, etc. Before flying you should check NOTAMs for your destination and the navigational aids that you will need *en route*. See page 68 for an occasion when a pilot didn't.

Oshkosh. Oshkosh is a small town in Wisconsin in the USA. Its claim to fame is that the US Experimental Aircraft Association (i.e., the association of pilots who build their own aircraft) has an air show there each year. This attracts thousands of aircraft ranging from small home-builts to Concordes. Many pilots plan their summer holidays around this show whether their families approve or not.

OTT. Over-The-Top. A rating which a Private Pilot can obtain which allows him or her to fly above a solid layer of cloud (not normally permitted in VFR flight) if the weather at the destination is likely to be good on arrival. A VFR-OTT pilot cannot fly *in* cloud but may climb through a gap in the cloud at the departure airfield, fly over an undercast and then descend through a gap at the destination. One obvious question is, "what if there isn't a gap in the cloud at the destination?" This is the reason that I personally believe the VFR-OTT rating is dangerous.

Overshoot. The act of deciding not to complete a landing, but instead to go around the circuit and make another approach. Perhaps another aircraft has moved out onto the runway, perhaps you don't feel comfortable about the approach. Sometimes called a "go-around." Even in the most macho of flying circles, an overshoot is considered a sensible rather than a wimpy thing to do if you're not comfortable with the approach.

Phonetic Alphabet. The words used to say letters over the radio. Thus to avoid confusion, the letters XBU would be said as X-RAY BRAVO UNIFORM. The most confusing letter is H, which is said as HOTEL although, in most anglophone and francophone countries, the H in HOTEL is silent.

Plates. This is the popular term for the pages in the Canada Air Pilot booklet.[20] Plates are designed primarily for pilots making instrument approaches to Canadian airports (i.e., pilots flying under the Instrument Flight Rules), but they are also of use to pilots flying VFR as they contain very clear runway and airport layouts. Like the *Canada Flight Supplement*, plates are issued roughly every 2 months, but unlike the *Canada Flight Supplement*, which covers the whole of Canada, plates are issued in 7 volumes covering different parts of the country.

Pre-flight Inspection. Before flying an aircraft, a pilot inspects it for obvious defects (for example, water in the fuel or insufficient oil). This is known as the pre-flight inspection.

PSTAR. An air-law examination which you have to take before you are allowed to fly solo.

Radial. A VOR navigation aid allows an aircraft to determine on what radial from the VOR it is currently flying: the 360 radials are numbered clockwise from 000 (north).

Runway Numbers. I once took someone flying from Rockcliffe who claimed that the airport was being pretentious numbering the ends of its runway 9 and 27, given that it only has the one runway. She thought that they should be called 1 and 2. Actually the runway number indicates its direction, add a zero and interpret it as a bearing: 000 being north, 090 being east, 180 being south and 270 being west. Thus Rockcliffe's runway 09/27 runs east/west. I explained this to the embarrassed passenger.

Stall. Nothing to do with the engine stopping: rather to do with the flow of air breaking away from the top of the aircraft's wing and the wing no longer producing lift.

TAF. Terminal Aerodrome Forecast. This is a weather forecast, typically valid for 24 hours, giving the meteorologists' best estimate for the wind speeds, cloud formations, etc., in a very small area around an airport. See the glossary entry for *METAR*.

Tail Dragger. Older aircraft all have their third, smaller, wheel under the tail: this is known as "conventional under-carriage" and such aircraft are known as Tail Draggers. Because their centre of gravity lies behind their main wheels, Tail Draggers are notoriously difficult to land in cross-winds since, if they arrive with any sideways motion caused by the wind, they will tend to turn into wind and leave the runway. Most training aircraft now have the third wheel under the nose and their centre of gravity lies in front of the main wheels. Any mistakes made in a cross-wind landing therefore cause the aircraft to try to straighten out along the runway. Real pilots, that is, pilots who fly Tail Draggers, tend to dismiss nose wheels as "training wheels."

Thermal. A thermal is one of the three main types of lift that a glider can use to gain height. A thermal is a column of rising air caused by some local heating on the ground. A field or road perhaps gets a few degrees hotter than its surroundings and the air above it starts to rise. A glider can circle in this rising air and be lifted thousands of feet. The other two main forms of lift are ridge lift (wind hitting a hill or ridge and being forced upwards) and wave lift (wind forming enormous waves in the air when it hits mountain ranges). Of these, wave lift is the most popular with glider pilots, since both thermals and ridge lift die out at a few thousand feet whereas wave lift can continue upwards to heights of over 30 000 feet.

Transponder. A device installed in an aircraft to allow Air Traffic Control to identify a particular aircraft on its radar screen. ATC will issue the aircraft with a unique 4-digit octal code (by saying "SQUAWK 1234") and the transponder returns this every time it is interrogated by radar.

Trim. Each time you fly an aircraft it requires slightly different control inputs to keep it in straight and level flight – caused primarily by different distributions of weight. In order to allow you to fly without continually pulling or pushing on the control column, most aircraft are fitted with Trim Tabs. These tabs are controlled from inside the cockpit (sometimes electrically, normally mechanically) and, when correctly adjusted, mean that the aircraft can be flown almost "hands-off."

UNICOM. Universal Communication. The frequently unattended radio at an uncontrolled airport. Since no permission is needed to land at or take off from an uncontrolled airport, you don't actually need to call the UNICOM, but when it is attended, the operator can advise on what the winds are doing and which runway to use. There is no requirement for a pilot to take the advice on which runway to use.

V Speeds. There are certain critical airspeeds associated with an aircraft and these are known as the *V Speeds*. The ones of interest to the general aviation pilot are:

- V_{ne}: the speed which the aircraft must never exceed. For a Diamond Katana, for example, this value is 161 knots.

- V_A: the highest speed at which you should make sudden control movements. This can also be thought of as the highest speed at which you can be sure that the aircraft will protect itself by stalling rather than come to structural harm. For a Katana this is 104 knots.

- V_{FE}: the highest speed at which the aircraft may be flown with the flaps down. For a Katana this value is 81 knots.

- V_X: the speed at which the aircraft gains the most height for the least forward motion. This is the speed you would use after takeoff if you had to clear a line of trees off the end of the runway. For a Katana this is 57 knots and results in a slow, steep climb.

- V_y: the speed at which the aircraft gains height as quickly as possible. If you are taking off from a runway without a row of trees at the end, then this is the most suitable climbing speed since it gets you to altitude as soon as possible. For a Katana this is 65 knots and results in a fast, shallow climb.

Most of these critical speeds are marked as colored bars on an aircraft's Airspeed Indicator.

VASIS. Visual Approach Slope Indicator System. Colored lights mounted beside the runways at larger airports to indicate whether you are too high or too low as you approach to land. If both lights appear white then you are too high. If they both appear red then you're too low. White over red means that you are just right.

VFR. Visual Flight Rules. The rules which you must follow if you do not have an Instrument Rating. The rules basically state that you must have the ground in sight at all times. See the glossary entry for IFR.

VMC. Visual Meteorological Conditions. The weather conditions under which VFR flight is allowed.

VNC. VFR Navigation Chart. The standard charts used for VFR Navigation within Canada. They have a scale of 1:500 000 and are available from all aviation shops and most map shops. See the glossary entry for VTA.

VOR. Very-High Frequency Omnidirectional Range. A radio transmitter that broadcasts a signal which allows a receiver in an aircraft to decide its direction to the transmitter.

VTA. VFR Terminal Area Chart. Most VFR navigation is performed using the so-called VNC charts. To help the VFR pilot flying close to a large airport, larger scale maps of the areas immediately around the airport are available – the VTAs. These maps have more detail to allow a pilot to keep out of controlled airspace and also mark VFR reporting points to be used when calling Air Traffic Control.

Useful Addresses

The Canadian Owners and Pilots Association (COPA).
1001-75 Albert St.,
Ottawa, Ontario, K1P 5E7.
Tel: 613-236-4901.
Email: copa@copanational.org
Web: http://www.copanational.org

The Canadian Precision Flying Association.
1000 Broken Oak Drive,
Orleans, Ontario, K1C 2W7

The Ninety-Nines,
The International Organization of Women Pilots.
Box 965, 7100 Terminal Dr.,
Oklahoma City, OK, 73159-0965, USA.
Tel: 405-685-7969.
Email: 99s@ninety-nines.org
Web: http://www.ninety-nines.org

The Recreational Aircraft Association.
Brampton Airport, R.R. #1,
Cheltenham, ON, L0P 1C0.
Toll-free: 1-800-387-1028.
Tel: 905-838-1357.
Email: raac@ inforamp.net
Web: http://www.inforamp.net/~raac

Experimental Aircraft Association Canadian Council.
2348 Garnet St.,
Regina, SK, S4T 3A2.
See http://www.eaa. org/chapters/directory/canadian.html for local chapters.

Canadian Seaplane Pilots Association.
1001-75 Albert St.,
Ottawa, ON, K1P 5E7.
Tel: 613-236-4901.
Email: info@canadianseaplane.com
Web: http://canadianseaplane.com

Air Combat Canada.

Niagara District Airport, Highway 55, R.R. #4,
Niagara-on-the-lake, ON, L0S 1J0.
Tel: 1-888-FLY-HARD(359-4273).
Email: operations@aircombatcanada.com
Web: http://www.aircombatcanada.com

Tomvale Air Services Ltd.

Tomvale Airport,
Ardoch, ON, K0H 1C0.
Tel: 613-479-2625.
Email: fly@ tomvale.on.ca
Web: http://www.tomvale.on.ca

References

[1] *Canada Flight Supplement* (Canada and North Atlantic Terminal and En Route Data), Transport Canada, Canada Map Office, Natural Resources Canada, 615 Booth St., Ottawa, ON K1A 0E9.

[2] *The Glider Pilot's Manual*, Ken Stewart. Published 1994 by Airlife Publishing Ltd., Shrewsbury, England.

[3] *Canadian Flight Annual*, Canadian Owners and Pilots Association (available either from the Canadian Owners and Pilots Association, 613-565-0881, or in many of the larger bookstores).

[4] *IFR, the magazine for the Accomplished Pilot*, Volume 13, Number 11 (November 1997) published by Belvoir Publications, 75 Holly Hill Lane, Greenwich, CT 06836-2626, USA.

[5] *Study Guide for the Radiotelephone Operator's Restricted Certificate (Aeronautical)*, Industry Canada document RIC-21.

[6] Student Pilot Permit or Private Licence for Foreign and Military Applicants, Aviation Regulation Examination, Transport Canada document PSTAR.

[7] *Aeronautical Information Publication*, Transport Canada Aviation document TP2300E.

[8] *Flight Guide, Airport and Frequency Manual*, Airguide Publications Inc., 1207 Pine Avenue, P.O. Box 1288, Long Beach, California, USA..

[9] *VFR Radio Procedures in the USA*, Published by RMC Inc. (+1-905-796-3066).

[10] *Canadian Flight Annual*, Canadian Owners and Pilots Association.

[11] *Fate is the Hunter*, Ernest K. Gann. Published 1986 by Simon & Schuster, New York.

[12]*Bush Pilot With a Briefcase*, Ronald A. Keith. Published 1997 by Douglas & McIntyre, Vancouver.

[13]*And I Shall Fly*, Z. Lewis Leigh. Published 1985, CANAV Books, Toronto.

[14]*Improve Your Flying Skills*, Donald J. Clausing. Published 1990, TAB Books, New York.

[15]*Flying the Weather Map*, Richard L. Collins. Published 1992 by Thomasson-Grant, Charlottesville, Virginia.

[16]*Meteorology and Flight*, Tom Bradbury. Published 1991 by A & C Black, London.

[17]*Aware, Aviation Weather . . . Playing by the Rules*, Environment Canada, Quebec Region.

[18]*Aeronautical Information Publication*, Transport Canada Aviation document TP2300E.

[19]*From the Ground Up*, Aviation Publishers Co. Ltd., Ottawa. Published 1996 (27th edition).

[20]*Canada Air Pilot, Instrument Procedures*, Geomatics Canada, Canada Map Office, Natural Resources Canada, 615 Booth St., Ottawa, ON K1A 0E9.

Index

Instrument Flight Rules (IFR), 28, 53, 67, 71, 73, 90, 93, 97

Instrument Landing System (ILS), 90

Instrument Meteorological Conditions (IMC), 28, 76, 91

Instrument Rating, 29-30, 41, 48, 63, 69, 74, 76, 96

landing, 7, 33-6, 38-9, 42, 47, 49-50, 59, 63, 74, 76, 84, 87, 90, 92

log books, 24, 33

magazines, 14, 25, 36, 63-5, 81, 83, 101

magnetic compass, 45, 51

maintenance, 17, 79

maps & charts, 19, 24, 45, 47, 49-50, 57, 63-5, 71, 75, 78, 85, 89, 97

mathematics, 12

Mayday, 42, 51, 91

medical, 10, 23-4, 27, 29-30

METAR, 91, 94

meteorology (see weather)

motion-sickness, 10

navigation, 9, 12-13, 19, 41, 44-50, 55, 62-3, 67-9, 71, 74-5, 77, 84-5, 91-3

NDB (Non-Directional Beacon), 19, 46-7, 49, 78, 91

Night Rating, 11, 30, 63

Ninety-Nines, 99

NOTAM (Notices to Airpersons), 68, 71, 92

Oshkosh, Wisconsin, 62, 92

overshoot, 49, 89, 92

phonetic alphabet, 51-2, 82, 93

poker run, 62

precision navigation competition, 50-1, 62

pre-flight inspection, 17, 35, 43-4, 68, 74, 93

Private Pilot Licence, 7, 13-14, 16, 18, 23-4, 27, 29-30, 41, 48-9, 53, 57-8, 60-1, 63-4, 92

Quebec, 15

radio, 11-12, 16, 19-20, 24, 27, 39, 41, 46-7, 51-2, 58, 67, 69-71, 77, 85, 88, 91, 93, 95, 97

Recreational Aircraft Association, 99

Recreational Permit, 13-14, 16, 18, 23-4, 27, 29-30, 48-9, 60

renting vs. owning aircraft, 17, 23-5

ridge lift, 95

Search and Rescue, 69, 88

slipping (skidding), 38